Other Titles in the Smart Pop Series

PERFECTLY

Unauthorized Essays on the Life, Loves,
and Other Disasters of
Stephanie Plum, Trenton Bounty Hunter

PLUM

Edited by
LEAH WILSON

BENBELLA BOOKS, INC.
Dallas, Texas

"Destiny: Disaster!" © 2007 by Bev Katz Rosenbaum
"Life on the Hamster Wheel" © 2007 by Tanya Michaels
"The 'N' in New Jersey Stands for Noir" © 2007 by Amy Garvey
"Exploding the Myth of the Jersey Girl" © 2007 by Devon Ellington
"Learning to Fly" © 2007 by Sylvia Day
"I Love Stephie" © 2007 by Carole Nelson Douglas
"Laughing Her Way Out of Trouble" © 2007 by Kyra Davis
"The Bad Boy Next Door" © 2007 by Shanna Swendson
"A Little Less Conversation" © 2007 by Donna Kauffman
"Eeny, Meeny, Miney, Mo" © 2007 by Nancy Tesler
"The Fast and the Furry-ous" © 2007 by Rhonda Eudaly
"The Gun in the Cookie Jar" © 2007 by Brenda Scott Royce
"From Disaster to Diva" © 2007 by Natasha Fondren
"Stephanie Plum's Trenton" © 2007 by Pam McCutcheon
"Could Stephanie Plum Really Get Car Insurance?" © 2007 by JA Konrath
"The Stephanie Plum Diet" © 2007 by Charlene Brusso
"Pineapple Upside-Down Cake" © 2007 by Candace Havens
"Why Can't You Be More Like Your Sister?" © 2007 by Keris Stainton
"Ranger as...Hairy Godmother?" © 2007 by Karen Kendall
Additional Materials © 2007 by BenBella Books

BenBella Books, Inc.
6440 N. Central Expressway, Suite 617
Dallas, TX 75206
www.benbellabooks.com
Send feedback to feedback@benbellabooks.com

Printed in the United States of America
10 9 8 7 6 5 4 3 2 1

Library of Congress Cataloging-in-Publication Data

Perfectly plum : unauthorized essays on the life, loves, and other disasters of Stephanie Plum, Trenton bounty hunter / edited by Leah Wilson.
    p. cm.
    ISBN 1-933771-04-6
    1. Evanovich, Janet—Characters—Stephanie Plum. 2. Evanovich, Janet—Criticism and interpretation. 3. Plum, Stephanie (Fictitious character) I. Wilson, Leah.

    PS3555.V2126Z84 2007
    813'.54—dc22

                                                                                            20070066

Proofreading by Emily Chauvier and Jennifer Thomason
Text design and composition by John Reinhardt
Cover design by Laura Watkins
Printed by Bang Printing

Distributed by Independent Publishers Group
To order call (800) 888-4741
www.ipgbook.com

For special sales contact Yara Abuata at yara@benbellabooks.com

CONTENTS

LIFE

LOVES

OTHER DISASTERS

LIFE

DESTINY: DISASTER!

Bev Katz Rosenbaum

Janet Evanovich begins One for the Money *by having Stephanie tell a story about Joe Morelli, a game of choo-choo, a pastry counter, and a Buick. It's the setup for her relationship with Morelli, of course, but it's also Stephanie in a nutshell: curious, rebellious, and not above taking a little well-earned revenge. Her core personality hasn't changed since she was seventeen. What if, Bev Rosenbaum asks, we could go further? What if, seeing Stephanie at seven years old, we could predict the course of the rest of her life?*

YOU WANNA TALK DISASTERS? Easy, where Stephanie Plum is concerned. A more disaster-prone woman never walked the earth. Okay, granted, she is a bounty hunter, and blown-up cars are part of the gig (though hers do seem to explode a good deal more than those of other law-enforcement types...like, in every book). Ditto hair accidents and destroyed clothing. But let's talk life-type disasters. Relationships, for example. The truth is, poor Stephanie never had a chance at a "normal" life. A cornucopia of genetic (can you say Grandma Mazur?) and environmental (regular working-class neighborhood, my arse) factors combined into a toxic soup that virtually guaranteed a disastrous adulthood for our favorite bail bondswoman.

Remember the famous "Up" documentary series (*7-Up*, *14-Up*, *21-Up*, etc), the premise of which was taken from the Francis Xavier quote and Jesuit motto, "Give me a child until he is seven and I will give you the man"? In the series, director Michael Apted interviewed the same group of people at ages seven, fourteen, twenty-one—I believe he's up to forty-nine now—to determine if they ended up living the lives they seemed destined for at age seven. I'm totally in love with the Up films, so I'm going to try to apply that same premise to the Stephanie Plum books, and demonstrate precisely how genetic and environmental factors, together with a seminal incident from her childhood, turned Stephanie Plum into the walking disaster we know and love. "Attempt" being the key word. Keep in mind that, as a novelist, I'm only a wannabe psychologist; I really have no idea which of the following laundry list of factors is responsible, in part or in whole, for how our beloved Stephanie turned out.

But while I'm no psychologist, I *am* somewhat of an expert on disaster-prone children and teens. As I said, I'm a novelist, and one who seems to specialize in odd, disaster-prone teenage heroines, possibly because of my own, er, colorful background. But my own childhood is the subject for a whole other essay in a whole other book. Or perhaps for a therapist's couch.

But I digress. Back to Stephanie we go. Let's talk family tree first. And let's begin with Stephanie's nutcase of a grandmother, the bony and bug-eyed Grandma Mazur who, when we first meet her in *One for the Money*, is coveting Stephanie's sexy black biker shorts. Grandma Mazur loves the action (particularly the, er, exciting viewings at Constantine Stiva's funeral parlor) and Stephanie, fortunately or unfortunately, depending on how you look at it, seems to share a special kinship with her loony *grandmère*. Possibly because Granny knows exactly how to push her daughter's buttons and loves to do so. (Like grandmother, like granddaughter.) Indeed, the two often team up against Stephanie's grimly determined-to-be-normal housewife mother Helen. Like when, say, Grandma Mazur wants to go to a viewing at Stiva's that Helen doesn't want her to go to. (And who can really blame her? Grandma Mazur has leapt on corpses, pried open closed coffins, and much, much worse at Stiva's.)

Which isn't to say Helen is completely normal herself. In fact, that almost psychopathic determination to lead a "normal" life, as evidenced by her on-the-clock dinner scheduling and constant food-related threats (she seems particularly to enjoy withholding pineapple upside-down cake) is practically a dead giveaway that the whole normalcy thing is a big act. Despite all her talk about how she'd love to engage in "regular" dinner table conversations as opposed to chat about guns and murder and such (and aliens, in the case of Grandma Mazur), Helen clearly possesses a violent streak herself. Witness the food fight she instigates in *Eleven on Top*.

It seems pretty clear to me that Helen is one of those women who married and had children because she had to. (By the way, I have a hunch Grandma Mazur was forced to suppress her craziness as a young and middle-aged woman, too. She is obviously reveling in her geriatric freedom to do and say whatever the hell she wants.) My feeling about Helen is (sort of) confirmed when, in *Seven Up*, Stephanie asks her mother if she ever gets tired of her life. Helen mutters a series of vague remarks before finally admitting she'd like to go back to school. Another telling detail: Helen develops a wee drinking problem in *Eleven on Top*. Though I suppose it's possible a wacko family like hers could drive anybody to drink. Doesn't necessarily mean she has regrets about what she's done—or not done—with her life. . . .

But it is a pretty safe guess that life as the disenchanted (i.e., bitter and crabby) Helen's kid was no picnic. And it's an equally good guess that Daddy Dearest did not make up for his wife's shortcomings. Fully retired at the beginning of the series, Stephanie's father now drives a cab, mostly to get away from his wife and mother-in-law. When he's at home, he spends most of his time grunting and cursing.

Helen's denial of her own sensibilities clearly backfired where her own child is concerned. But who wouldn't rebel against such a dour version of "normal" life? Under the circumstances, it's hardly surprising that Stephanie's childhood aspirations included becoming an intergalactic princess and marrying, not the son of the neighborhood plumber like her best friend Mary Lou, but Aladdin.

How interesting that in *To the Nines*, Stephanie admits that, like her sister Valerie, she, too, longs to be rescued. Dare I suggest that perhaps Stephanie never really wanted this crazy life she's chosen for herself? That she felt she *had* to lead an, um, unusual life because the alternative (i.e., Helen's life) was just too horrible to contemplate?

And seeing as we've mentioned Stephanie's sister Valerie . . .

Here is another Plum woman Stephanie obviously could not bear to emulate. Valerie was the Perfect Daughter, who grew up into the Perfect Wife and Mother—although clearly, a latent wild streak ran deep in the Talbots-clad Valerie, who was so good for so long that something in her snapped when her "perfect" husband in California left her for a teenager. Now back in the Burg along with her two daughters—one preternaturally smart, and another who thinks she's a horse—Valerie's become just as crazy as Stephanie, considering a bounty hunter career like hers, and getting knocked up by a decidedly strange child-man named Kloughn (giving Valerie the perfect excuse for her mood swings and general weirdness: hormones).

Perhaps it's not such a coincidence that Valerie feels free to let out the wild woman in her once she's back in the Burg. The very place seems to not only encourage but require its inhabitants to be wild and/or weird, *à la* Stephanie. Some people believe that peers have just as much influence, if not more, on how a child turns out than a child's family, and when I consider the people the Plum girls were surrounded with from birth in the Burg, I must say, I'm inclined to agree.

New Jersey itself is bad enough. As Stephanie's co-worker Connie Rosolli says, "The way I see it, living in New Jersey is a challenge, what with the toxic waste and the 18-wheelers and the armed schizophrenics. I mean, what's one more lunatic shooting at you?" (*One for the Money* 16). But the Burg, that specific and strangely wonderful blue-collar chunk of Trenton, is a neighborhood unlike any other. . . .

Naturally, the Burg boasts a goodly selection of lowlifes and criminals with colorful names such as Skoogie and Moogey and Cookie and Cubbie. But even the most seemingly ordinary of citizens in the Burg are, um, interesting specimens of humanity. Stephanie's boss (and cousin) Vinnie is a not-so-closeted sadomasochist whose taste runs to "pointy-breasted women and dark-skinned young men" (*One for the Money* 16), and who is rumored to have done unspeakable (sexual) things to a duck. One of Stephanie's love interests, Ranger (a "real" bounty hunter), has a shadowy background in . . . well, we're not quite sure. Stephanie's friend and coworker Lula is a former prostitute, and the neighborhood school bus driver, Sally Sweet, is a drag queen of monstrous proportions, in addition to being an aspiring rock musician.

Now consider the community's elderly population. There are old ladies who have dark visions (*à la* Joe Morelli's Grandma Bella), others with Godfather complexes (like the terrifying Mama Macaroni, owner of Kan Klean Cleaners), and the rest are self-medicated, TV-addicted zombies.

Consider, too, the housewives. In the Burg, it's not at all uncommon for women to catfight in shoe stores, or to discuss the merits of certain gun brands over others while picking out nail polish colors at the beauty parlor. In *Four to Score*, a co-worker of Stephanie's recruits her housewife cousin to help out with a takedown. In other working-class neighborhoods, a housewife looking for something to do might consider selling Avon beauty products. Not so in the Burg.

In fact, it's not at all difficult to imagine the housewives themselves becoming the criminals. Actually, in *Four to Score*, this is exactly what happens. Betty Glick, when ordering her husband to kill their hostage, says, "And don't make a mess. I just cleaned down there. Choke her like you did Nathan. That worked out good" (280).

It isn't just the housewives who are obsessed with guns and death. It's the entire community. There's no bingo in the Burg. Instead, showings at the funeral parlor pack 'em in. (Grandma Mazur is by no means the only interested party.) At one point in *Four to Score*, Joe's Grandma Bella describes a relative's death from cancer in overly graphic detail to Stephanie, happily adding once she's done that she hopes Stephanie enjoys the casserole she's brought over.

Life in the Burg, as Janet Evanovich depicts it, is Americana Surreal. Ordinary life times a thousand. The right to bear arms becomes the right to blow away anybody who ticks you off. Similarly, individualizing your semi-detached home may entail, not just planting a few flowers or erecting a pretty picket fence, but painting it bright turquoise and adorning it with a full array of Christmas lights and a five-foot-tall plastic Santa strapped to a rusted TV antenna (Louie Moon's house, reverently described in *Two for the Dough*). In the parking lot of the local chicken joint, Cluck in a Bucket, a seven-foot-tall plastic chicken is "impaled" (Evanovich's word) on a rotating pole (*Three to Get Deadly* 224).

The whole place is terrifyingly bizarre—and 100 percent made in America. Growing up in the Burg, with all its weirdness, virtually guaranteed that Stephanie Plum, already doomed as the descendant of a long line of crazies, didn't have a ghost of a chance of becoming a "normal" adult.

Then, of course, there is *the* seminal event of Stephanie's childhood. I don't think it's a coincidence that *One for the Money* opens with Stephanie describing an incident that took place when she was six years old: the game of "choo-choo" she was "coerced" into playing by Joe Morelli (one of the "wild" Morelli boys her mother had warned her about, with whom Stephanie was then compelled to become involved). It's pretty clear that Stephanie, while a tad confused about the encounter, um, enjoyed playing the game. So much so that a decade later, she allowed Joe to take her virginity behind the éclair case of Tasty Pastry, where she worked part-time after school.

Clearly, once Stephanie tasted the wild life, she was hooked—although she wasn't necessarily happy about it. (Three years after the Tasty Pastry incident, she decided to hit Joe with her car when she saw him walking in the street. A delayed reaction, perhaps, to the choo-choo incident—the guy seduced her when she was *six!*—as much as to the, er, cavalier way in which he took her virginity.)

Now in her late twenties, Stephanie is still wildly attracted to Joe, but it's become increasingly clear he isn't quite the rebel he used to be. While still gorgeous and sexy, he's loyal to Stephanie, takes good care of his dog Bob, and seems open to the idea of being a husband and father.

So naturally, Stephanie, in a reflex reaction to the horrifying specter of a domestic life (memories of Helen!) has gone and risked screwing everything up by (sort of) becoming involved with Ranger, the super-tough mystery man with the shadowy past.

Why settle for a great relationship with a normal guy—who, as a cop, leads almost as action-packed a life as Ranger—when you can engage in a dangerous game of Risk-Losing-Them-Both?

Anyone who's tooled around the Internet in the wake of a bad breakup recognizes all the signs of a commitment phobe in Stephanie. Sabotaging a relationship is a bright glowing green symptom. Ditto uncertainty about committing to a future with even the most fabulous of guys. So is engaging in a relationship with someone who may be interested in a physical but not necessarily intimate relationship (Ranger's work and lifestyle do not exactly scream "soccer dad").

Let this author just take a moment to say that, despite all her posturing about Stephanie being a crazy commitment phobe who's totally screwing up her chance at something great with Morelli by engaging in something on the side with Ranger, she, too, would probably have a great deal of difficulty choosing between Morelli and Ranger, as, indeed, would any normal, warm-blooded female....

But back to commitment-phobic behavior. It isn't strictly relegated to relationships. It can also involve school and jobs. How fascinating, in that light, is Stephanie's college and employment history. Our girl graduated with self-admitted mediocre grades from Douglass

College, after which she worked as a lingerie buyer for a cheap department store for a bunch of years before she got laid off when her employer's mob connections (which our troubled heroine probably knew about) became public. She went to work for Vinnie for a while, then quit in order to try her hand at an assortment of other disastrous jobs (at a button factory, where she was promptly fired on her first day for being late; at Kan Klean, for the terrifying Mama Macaroni; and then at Cluck in a Bucket, where she started a fire while attempting to thwart a bomb someone gave her—don't ask), eventually going back to Vinnie.

Authors, as I've mentioned, are amateur shrinks par excellence. And we, like all those other amateur Internet shrinks, are all too aware that commitment-phobic behavior is associated with a fear of rejection and is firmly rooted in one's childhood.

Helen made her disapproval of Stephanie loud and clear from the time Stephanie was a young girl, and continues to do so, in spite of her own secret (and possibly only in this author's head) longing for a wild life. It's no wonder that Stephanie distances herself from others in order to protect herself, and commits to no job.

And while we're playing amateur shrink...

Just as it's no surprise that, given her childhood role models, Stephanie is a classic commitment phobic, it isn't exactly a shock to learn that she's formed a junk-food addiction, doughnuts being her "drug" of choice. Sugar, it's been proven, affects the production of dopamine endorphins in the brain. In layman's terms, Stephanie uses junk food to make her feel better.

Or maybe she just likes junk food.

And maybe, like I said, she truly just can't choose between Morelli and Ranger.

Maybe she's not such a disaster, after all.

She *is* super-cool, you have to admit—brave as well as loyal (she still shows up for those family dinners, and she did give Valerie and the clown—I mean, Albert Kloughn—her apartment when Helen had a meltdown).

Maybe we just like to label unconventional people, call them weird, disaster-prone. Maybe instead of labeling people like Stephanie, we should aspire to be more like them. You have to admit, the world would certainly be a more interesting place with more Stephanies around.

Which isn't to say we should try our best to ensure our kids grow up like Stephanie. But maybe we should all just . . . relax a bit. Anybody see that *Gilmore Girls* episode with Emily training all the little girls for the cotillion? Emily's daughter Lorelai, whose relationship with her mother is much like Stephanie's with Helen, forms a connection with one mischievous sprite who wears Converse sneakers with her fancy, crinolined dress. Like Stephanie, unconventional Lorelai, who got knocked up as a teen but has proven to be a world-class mother and all around great human being, could well serve as a kickass female role model.

Wonder what Stephanie Plum would be like as a mother?

Now there's something I'd love to see. Would she have a little clone who would exasperate her, as she did (and still does) her own mother, or a girl who would rebel by going to grandma's for cooking lessons? (Wouldn't blame the kid for that. Helen's full of fabulous meatloaf tips, which she usually voices in a strangled monotone while attempting to change the subject from attempted murder.)

But maybe that can wait for a few more books. Stephanie may not be a disaster, but she could certainly stand to work out a few, um, issues.

The child is the woman, indeed. . . .

A former fiction and magazine editor, **BEV KATZ ROSENBAUM** is the author of the young adult novels *I Was a Teenage Popsicle* and its upcoming sequel *Beyond Cool*. She doesn't think she's quite as messed up as Stephanie Plum, but it's certainly close. Bev lives in Toronto with her husband and two children.

LIFE ON THE HAMSTER WHEEL

Tanya Michaels

It's one of the difficulties of long-running series: you want things to change, because you don't want your audience to get bored, but you don't want things to change too much and lose what the audience loved about the series in the first place. So Stephanie sometimes seems like she's going around in circles—vacillating between Joe and Ranger, never really getting better at bounty hunting, still living pretty much the same life she was living at the end of book one. All that running around getting nowhere reminds Tanya Michaels of something. . . . Oh, right. Rex's hamster wheel.

MANY OF US WHO ENJOY returning to the world of Stephanie Plum do so not just because we love Stephanie, but because hers is a world full of colorful characters. It's one hell of a rogues' gallery, from two strong Alpha male heroes to quirky Grandma Mazur, from larger-than-life Lula to nemesis Joyce Barnhardt and the bad guys who invariably want Stephanie dead. Yet ironically, with all these people surrounding Steph, it's the smallest character, the one who never says anything at all, who speaks volumes about her life: Rex the hamster.

For members of different species, Stephanie and Rex share an uncanny number of similarities. Neither of them likes hamster pellets, which Stephanie admits to having tried for breakfast (*One for the Money* 13), but they both love Butterscotch Krimpets, Helen Plum's pineapple upside-down cake, Pino's pizza, and a host of other foods. (Rex, of course, has the healthier diet of the two since he frequently eats the raisins, grapes, apple chunks, and carrots that Steph keeps in the fridge for him.) Stephanie has days where she feels like crawling back into bed and hiding from reality; Rex often retreats to his soup can. Like his owner, Rex harbors some affection for Morelli (who's been known to feed him on occasion—love and food are pretty closely intertwined in the Burg). Both bounty hunter and hamster lead a somewhat nomadic lifestyle, with Steph's apartment serving as sort of a central, frequently broken-into base, as Stephanie, with Rex more often than not in tow, drifts between other locations such as her increasingly crowded childhood home, Morelli's house, and, for a brief period in *Ten Big Ones*, an apartment of Ranger's.

Still, these are mostly superficial resemblances. The more meaningful, and sometimes puzzling, similarity is that both Rex and Stephanie have *survived* for so many books. I love Stephanie and would certainly never wish her ill (even if I do envy the devotion of two incredibly sexy men and her ability to zip jeans and wear short skirts in spite of atrocious eating habits). But you have to admit, it's statistically improbable that one untrained young woman could survive multiple car-bombings, kidnapping, the death wishes of a homicidal rapist, serial killers, gang members with a contract out on her life, and, just to top it all off, the Garden State garden-variety ill will of armed and aggressive FTAs who don't care to be in custody. As Morelli, Ranger, and Stephanie herself have all repeatedly pointed out, Stephanie's main skill as a bounty hunter—and, next to fibbing, her *only* skill—is luck. She attributes this in part to her Hungarian heritage and gypsy intuition (*Ten Big Ones* 2). Steph's the bond enforcement equivalent of an idiot savant.

Rex, unlike his owner, isn't out making enemies, but he still pays a dangerous price for being the only other member of her tiny household. While Stephanie is off losing handcuffs and watching various vehicles go up in flames, Rex faces his own problems at home. In *Two for the Dough*, he is locked in his aquarium with an angry cat; in *Three to Get Deadly*, crazed vigilantes are prepared to shoot him full of drugs and let him overdose in order to make a brutal point; in *Four to Score*, he is alone in the apartment when it is set on fire. Is it just me, or is impending death something of an unfortunate pattern for the dark-eyed little fella?

Then again, in another instance of hamster-mirroring-heroine, Rex employs some of the exact same modes of protection that Stephanie does: no small amount of luck and animalistic survival instincts, for starters. Despite lacking street smarts, Stephanie has enough primitive drive to kill Jimmy Alpha, saving her own life in *One for the Money*, long before she has to shoot Clyde Cone in *To the Nines*.

Smaller but fierce when the occasion calls for it, Rex has been known to sink his fangs into the bad guy, then escape under the couch (*Three to Get Deadly* 293).

Actually, while Rex does the actual biting, his escape in this instance is a team effort. Stephanie stalls the hamster execution with something of a hysterical meltdown, knowing exactly what will happen if she gives Rex time. Which leads us to that other source of protection they share—love. I don't think it's overstating things to say that Stephanie would run into a burning building to carry out her hamster; she is on the verge of exactly that in *Four to Score*, but it turns out to be unnecessary since some neighbors have already saved him. Stephanie demonstrates her devotion time and again. When Stephanie is kidnapped by men who plan to systematically dismember her to draw Ranger out in *Hot Six*, one of the first things she does after escaping is call Morelli and ask him to protect her hamster. She looks out for the little guy, even in times of crisis. Correction, *especially* in times of crisis.

Perhaps not coincidentally, Stephanie has her own motley network of people who look out for her. Even unlikely candidates with less street-smarts and training than Stephanie herself can save the day with enough motivation—witness Grandma Mazur, who gains the advantage over apprentice undertaker Spiro Stiva and his psychotic colleague Kenny in *Two for the Dough* when she whips out her .45. In *Four to Score*, it's Lula's phone call to the police that leads to eventual rescue after Stephanie once again enacts the stall-for-time ploy. Hairy transvestite and musician Sally Sweet rides to the rescue in a school bus and saves her life, despite Stephanie's expressly stated lack of confidence that he'll succeed. Even dutiful Burg housewife Helen Plum, known for crossing herself when alarmed and ironing when stressed, can be lethal when it comes to protecting her daughter. In *Hard Eight*, with the help of an accelerating LeSabre, Helen kills one of the stalkers who had been trying to kidnap Stephanie. This dramatic intervention by a loved one foreshadows the end of the book, when it's strongly implied that Ranger, one of two men in love with Stephanie, hunts the bad guy down and kills him to protect her. Indirectly complicit is the *other* man who loves her, Joe Morelli, whose job is upholding the law but who nonetheless looks the other way. Sure, Stephanie may be gifted with luck and intuition, but equally responsible for her survival are two very skilled, very dangerous men who have killed for her and would probably take a bullet for her as well.

With this kind of back-up from family, lovers, and various oddball friends consistently demonstrated book after book, it makes Stephanie's comment to Albert Kloughn that "I usually work alone" (*Hard Eight* 88) seem ungrateful, if not downright delusional. She's gone out in the field with Lula, Ranger, Tank, Vinnie—even Bob the dog, who was instrumental in taking down hit man Leon James in *Twelve Sharp*. But there's more to Stephanie's "alone" statement than merely her trying to wiggle out of taking Kloughn along on a bust. Deep down, being a loner is one more thing Stephanie and Rex have in common.

The hamster spends all his time cooped up in an aquarium, devoid of the companionship of a lady hamster or even hamster buddies to come over to run on the wheel with him. This seems okay with him, as he retreats into his soup can for even further solitude and doesn't like to be handled. In *Two for the Dough*, Rex literally bites the hand that feeds him, prompting Stephanie not only to release him but inadvertently fling him away. In the next book, Stephanie acknowledges to herself, when setting up the bad guy to be bitten, "I was watching Rex, because I knew what would happen if he was held long enough" (*Three to Get Deadly* 292).

While Stephanie doesn't live in a literal aquarium, she creates her own walls and boundaries, only letting people in for a brief time. Her marriage to Dickie Orr is on record as one of the Burg's shortest; she couldn't even commit to keeping Bob, instead preferring to turn him over to Joe and visit occasionally. Granted, Dickie's doing the wild thing on the dining room table with Joyce Barnhardt is reasonable grounds for divorce. And it would be tough to keep a dog Bob's size in an apartment all day even if he *weren't* eating the furniture. But her pattern of temporary relationships doesn't stop with ex-husband and golden retriever.

Although a pretty good liar when it comes to fibbing to others, one of Stephanie's more admirable traits is her honesty with herself. She can admit that she likes her own space and unchallenged control of the television remote. Consider her parade of short-lived (two-legged) roommates: she and Morelli have an on-again, off-again cohabitation;

angry little person and computer whiz Randy Briggs takes up residence in her apartment until he decides it's too dangerous to live there; Grandma Mazur moves in just long enough to thwart Steph's sex life and make Morelli crazy with frustration; Mooner Dunphy crashes on her couch until he's kidnapped; and Ranger uses her apartment as a safe house in *Twelve Sharp*, reciprocating Stephanie's moving in with him in *Ten Big Ones*. Most of the books, though, end with Stephanie back in her own home, roommate-free and alone once again.

A notable exception to this rule is when she sub-lets her apartment to her sister Valerie toward the end of *To the Nines*, so that Valerie, Albert, and the three girls have more room. Before we're even halfway into *Ten Big Ones*, however, Stephanie pushes an argument with Joe, fully acknowledging to herself that "I was working my way out of Morelli's house" (103). Technically, this occurs after she picks a fight by driving home in Ranger's truck. I say "picks" because she knows what's going to happen and proceeds anyway: "Morelli wouldn't be happy about me going off with Lula, but he'd understand.... The truck was going to provoke a full-blown contest of wills" (*Ten Big Ones* 99). If it hadn't been that particular fight, it would have been something else—while living with Morelli for several months had proven "surprisingly easy" (*Ten Big Ones* 47), Stephanie often misses her apartment. She's warning Joe of trouble to come when she tells him that she misses her independence, or at least her own bathroom. Even in the previous book, while she's still happily living with Morelli, Stephanie Freudian slips by driving to her apartment building before realizing her so-called mistake (*To the Nines* 91).

When Steph moves out in *Ten Big Ones*, it's déjà vu all over again, mirroring their *Seven Up* break up where she leaves after Joe issues an ultimatum during a fight. No self-respecting woman is going to take an ultimatum well, particularly a Jersey girl who's been known to carry assorted weapons, but once again Stephanie is self-aware enough to know her leaving isn't simply a response to his ill-timed macho demand. Once she's out of Morelli's presence, she realizes that "We're finding ways to sabotage the relationship" (*Seven Up* 303). Insightful, but as time passes, it begins to look as if the saboteur is Stephanie herself. While Morelli has his faults, it's Stephanie who, like her hamster, tends to bite when held too long.

One arguably major difference between Stephanie and Rex is exercise.

Rex spends lots of time on his wheel, while Stephanie normally only runs when prodded by Ranger or Morelli…or when people with guns chase her. Still, she spends as much time jogging in circles and getting nowhere as her small furry friend. Stephanie is living her life on an invisible hamster wheel.

The books in the Stephanie Plum series take place over a series of *years*, and many of the people living around her reflect that time lapse, changing and evolving. Lula gives up prostitution to file in Vinnie's office and eventually takes night classes; while the band she and Sally form in *Twelve Sharp* might never be a raging success, at least she's always looking for ways to expand her horizons. Equally colorful Grandma Mazur decides to dive back into the dating pool and even earns her driver's license (though it is quickly revoked, making the streets of Trenton a little safer). Saint Valerie, Stephanie's "perfect" sister, moves back home from California a single mother, and attempts to embrace change by trying to be a lesbian. That doesn't work out, but she does get involved with Albert Kloughn and have his baby. The changes in Morelli's life are slower, more subtle, but he does inherit and move into his aunt's house and begin to make it his own. He also ends up a dog-owner, and buys an uncharacteristic SUV to better accommodate said dog. Even Ranger is given different facets over time. Whether he's actually changing or simply allowing Stephanie to see more sides of him, the change in our perception of him still denotes the progress of his feelings for Stephanie, which is most profoundly articulated when his biological daughter is kidnapped: "I've kept myself emotionally distanced," Ranger tells Stephanie. "I'm *not* emotionally distanced from *you*" (*Twelve Sharp* 204).

While everyone around her has been developing feelings and making changes, Stephanie is much as she was when we first met her: a woman who lives alone, glad she has a hamster instead of kids despite periodic maternal pangs, as she makes her way through the world of fugitive apprehension with little more than stubbornness and blind luck. Although she quits her bond-enforcement job in *Eleven on Top*, this can't be considered a real change—it's more an impulsive reaction based on annoyance, much like her walking away from Morelli mid-discussion. Quitting turns out to be as temporary as the time Steph went blonde and almost immediately resolved to have Mr. Alexander change it back in *Seven Up*. Also, during her brief flirtation with other kinds of employment, people still want her dead, she and Lula still do takedowns, and vehicles continue to blow up left and right. So the status quo is pretty well maintained. Stephanie's life remains a circle of exploding cars, family dinners, and memorial viewings—even though Stiva's has to be rebuilt after she burns it down, and even though the funeral home passes to new ownership in *Twelve Sharp* after Con becomes a con in Rahway.

When we first meet Stephanie Plum in *One for the Money*, she tells us about Joe Morelli, how she slept with him once at sixteen and later hit him with her dad's Buick. This set a precedent for their relationship that hasn't changed as much as one might expect over the years, although there's now the added complication of Ranger, and now Stephanie normally just makes a hand-gesture and leaves rather than running Joe over. The truth is, Stephanie is in love with Joe. She's able to admit it to herself and to the reader, although she can't bring herself to voice it, even though he habitually tells her he loves her. When Stephanie comes face to face for the first time with Junkman, a hired killer, two of her immediate thoughts are that she doesn't want Rex to be an orphan and that she regrets never telling Morelli that she loves him (*Ten Big Ones* 244). But when she later has a chance to rectify that omission, she can't say it. Even in the next book, after more time has passed, the best she manages by way of response is "'I...l-l-like you, too.' *Shit*" (*Eleven On Top* 169) and "'I l-l-l-like you, too.' *Shit*" (*Eleven On Top* 250).

While Ranger is definitely an appealing figure, and it's easy to see how he could make a red-blooded woman's knees weak, Stephanie knows she'll never have a true relationship with him. Yet the times she pushes him away are half-hearted at best. Like when she tells him he's poaching and should stop: "'You don't mean that,' Ranger said, smiling. He was right" (*Ten Big Ones* 72). I suspect, for all Steph's thoughts about the complicated dilemma of choosing between two attractive and willing men, not only is part of her sincerely attracted to Ranger, part of her is *relieved* to have him as a wedge between herself and Joe. Because now she has a semi-convenient justification for not committing to Morelli. Even Ranger himself tells her, "I'm seeing an unhealthy pattern of behavior here, Babe" (*Ten Big Ones* 253).

Rex represents both the best and worst of Stephanie's life. The fact that she even has a pet shows her caring, nurturing side. She's loyal and loving, generally looks out for others, and always returns to her family or agrees to ride along with Lula even though she knows disaster will probably ensue. But the fact that the biggest responsibility she's willing to take on is a hamster shows her inability to throw herself fully into a relationship. Even among family and friends, it's not uncommon for Steph to develop an eye-twitch and want to take off for parts unknown and solitary. She has snuck out of family dinners as often as she's walked out on Joe, and even after a dozen books, Lula's only rated as a "sometimes-partner" (*Twelve Sharp* 2) and Morelli as a "sort of" boyfriend (*Twelve Sharp* 16).

Hamsters aren't expected to do a lot of personal growth, so Rex can be forgiven this somewhat limited character arc. Stephanie, however, seems like too intelligent a woman to make the same mistakes indefinitely and continue waffling indecisively. Though she's expressed unhappiness with her job and her life, the only changes she's tried to make have been either superficial (her hair), brief (her employment), or fictional (the whopping lie that she could play the cello, just so her family would think her life consisted of something more than "blowing up cars and trucks and funeral parlors and people" [*Eleven On Top* 112]). Stephanie is smart and has a history of eventually being honest with herself, whether or not she likes the truth. At some point, she will either have to make some changes or accept things the way they are. Which might also include accepting that she will never have a real relationship with Morelli *or* Ranger.

To give Steph credit where it's due, at the conclusion of *Twelve Sharp*, she is finally able to tell Morelli that she loves him (305). Maybe this means that she has grown as a heroine, that she's put the worst of her indecisiveness and inability to choose behind her. Then again, considering her very next thought after the admission is, "What wasn't said was that I also loved Ranger" (305), maybe not.

Almost all of us have trouble adjusting our habits and eradicating our flaws, so it stands to reason that Stephanie has grappled with some of the same issues book after book. Will thirteen be her lucky number, where she's able to make up her mind, make some improvements to her life, and avoid having a vehicle explode anywhere in her vicinity? I don't know. But I'm confident that no matter what happens—in spite of any of their flaws, compulsive eating tendencies, or occasionally anti-social behavior—Rex and Stephanie will live to triumph another day. Just as I'm confident that they will always have people who love them, look after them, and keep them well-fed.

TANYA MICHAELS is the award-winning author of more than a dozen romance and women's fiction novels. Uncoordinated to the point of accident-prone, yet at other times unbelievably lucky, Tanya relates to Stephanie Plum. There are occasionally days when being a writer feels as grueling as being a bounty hunter, but, on the upside, Tanya's minivan has never exploded. She makes her real home in Georgia with her husband and children, and her cyberhome at www.tanyamichaels.com.

THE "N" IN NEW JERSEY
STANDS FOR NOIR

Amy Garvey

*Noir. It's a genre full of down-on-their-luck private eyes solv-
ing morally oblique cases and resisting the temptations of
mysterious dames with great gams. Stephanie Plum would fit
right in. No? Well, Amy Garvey says, actually....*

I'M A CARD-CARRYING, lifelong book addict. If you catch me out
and about minus a book in my bag, it's a sure sign the world is ending. Even so, there are a lot of books out there, you know? (And
I *do* know, because some days it seems like half of them are in the
towering to-be-read pile, more correctly called a tower, that lives in
my bedroom. And has spawned several offspring in other parts of
the house.) Somehow, despite the fact that I lived for nine years just
across the river from Trenton and love kick-ass heroines, it took me
a while to find Stephanie Plum.

I'm not sure what I was expecting. Fun, certainly. A little romance,
a little sex, a little action, all of which are right up my alley when it
comes to a good read. I mean, how can you go wrong with a female
bounty hunter trying to manage both her love life and the criminal
element? But after I dug in deeper, I realized I'd found something
with a whole lot more meat to it than the pop-art bright covers and
catchy titles suggested. I'd found a twisted, funny as hell take on the
time-honored noir genre—and I loved it.

What's noir? *Noir* means "black" in French, and that's really the
best place to start. Noir *is* black, and not only because the original
films that defined the genre were shot in black and white. Noir is an
attitude—and we all know Stephanie and the other denizens of the
Plumverse have that in spades.

But it's not a sunny attitude. A laundry list of influences and world events—including painting and literature, German Expressionism, and a couple of other European "–isms"—came together to create what we think of as noir, but its visual style is always the first clue, at least when it comes to film. Ever see the black-and-white commercial for Flonase with the detective in the fedora and the dame in distress? Noir influence, right there.

The giants of the genre are some of film's true classics: *The Maltese Falcon, Laura, The Big Sleep, Key Largo, Double Indemnity.* Think shadows, both metaphorical and literal, as well as secrets, lies, deception, and usually more than one dead body or crime. Think edgy, gritty, and not terribly nice, a world peopled with folks whose morals are as flexible as overcooked spaghetti, and one in which the endings aren't always—or even usually—what anyone would call happy.

For example, in *Laura*, a police detective investigates the murder of a beautiful young woman and begins to fall in love with her as he pieces together her short life. Obviously, no recipe for happiness there—especially when he discovers this particular murder, as well as its victim, is not exactly what it seems.

The *femme fatale* to beat all *femmes fatales* is the key to *Double Indemnity*. Barbara Stanwyck plays a double-crossing beauty who lures an insurance salesman into an affair—as well as a murderous insurance scam.

As counterpoints to other famous movies of the 1940s—films such as *It's a Wonderful Life, Yankee Doodle Dandy*, and *The Philadelphia Story*— these noir classics couldn't have been more perfect. Noir is the film negative of the "feel good" movie, what a cynical, sherry-swilling spinster aunt is to a bubbly teenager in pastel sweater sets and a flippy ponytail. Which is partly why I love it—in movies as well as books, I adore fantasy happy endings (think *The Princess Bride* or *Pretty Woman* or any number of deliciously frothy romances), but once in a while I need to ignore my sweet tooth and order a fiery, no-frills scotch, neat. That's what noir is—a look, not at how the world could be, if it were perfect and the good guys always won and the guy got the girl (or vice versa), but at how the world too often *is*. Despite the black-and-white film technique, noir is all about those inconvenient, all-too-realistic shades of gray.

And all of this has what, exactly, to do with Stephanie's world, you say? The Plumverse isn't set in the forties or fifties, for one, and it's a series of books, not movies! I know, I know. Just wait.

First of all, noir's not dead. Remember the Flonase commercial? Noir influence lives on, and sometimes in very surprising places. *Memento*, *Fargo*, *The Usual Suspects*, and *Angel Heart* are all good examples of modern noir movies. Remember, it's all in the attitude. And even though *Angel Heart* could just as easily be filed under "horror," and *Fargo* is far funnier than any classic film noir from the 1940s— not to mention set in the frozen, down-home landscape of North Dakota, instead of L.A. or New York—both films are dead-on examples of the genre's influence. No, uh, pun intended.

An even more unlikely homage to noir can be found right on your TV screen, in the form of Rob Thomas's brilliant *Veronica Mars*. On the surface, it doesn't look anything like noir—it's set in the sun-drenched, surf-and-style town of Neptune on the California coast. The PI in question is no hardboiled older man with too many bottles of Jim Beam under his belt and too many run-ins with double-crossing dames to count. No, the PI is Veronica herself, a teenage girl who wields a mean telescoping camera, carries a taser, and uncovers Neptune's slimy underbelly on a regular basis. Veronica is a new-wave Nancy Drew—one who is less interested in Ned than in who murdered her best friend—and one who knows that truly happy endings, especially in her hometown, are few and far between.

Sound familiar yet?

I could give you examples of the lengthy, fabled history of noir fiction, too—the hardboiled school of detectives that included Raymond Chandler's Phillip Marlowe and Dashiell Hammett's Sam Spade, and the novels of James Ellroy (whose *L.A. Confidential* became another classic neo-noir film)—but I think you get the picture. The simple version is this: if women are called "broads" or "dames" and have great gams, and the men smoke and wear hats, chances are you're reading noir fiction.

What you want to know is why I think the Plumverse is another example of noir, right? Well, actually I don't, not exactly. What I do think is that Janet Evanovich brilliantly twisted the noir tropes into something that's partly an homage to the genre and partly a subversion of it, written with tongue-in-cheek humor and a lot of heart. You have to look closely, but the key aspects of noir are all right there. They're simply turned on their heads, and sometimes sideways and backwards.

No matter what the plot entails—and there are noir films ranging in storyline from a bankrupt hack writing a comeback screenplay for a fading silent screen star (*Sunset Boulevard*) to friends who find millions of dollars in the cockpit of a downed plane (*A Simple Plan*)— noir usually shares a few key characteristics. And the Stephanie Plum series features most of them, if not exactly in the way you might expect.

Wikipedia says, "Film noir tends to revolve around flawed and desperate characters in an unforgiving world." Now that sounds familiar. When we first meet Stephanie, she may not be quite as flawed as she believes, but she is nothing short of desperate. Laid off from her job as a lingerie buyer, as *One for the Money* opens Stephanie is late on her car payments, making deals with the repo guy, and has nothing more in her fridge than hamster nuggets, a bottle of beer, and some crusty condiments. Desperate? I think so, too. But Stephanie's desperation, while real enough, is also—let's face it—kind of funny. Stephanie hasn't lost a beloved spouse, she's not bent on the brand of personal vengeance that so often motivates noir protagonists—she's pissed off that someone's going to take her Miata away, and there is no way in hell she's moving back into her parents' house.

And if her world is unforgiving, it's unforgiving in the way only modern society can be. As Stephanie herself is the first to point out, her former employer wasn't exactly Victoria's Secret—how could it be, located in that epitome of New Jersey mean streets, Newark? (Which is, for the uninitiated, pronounced something like *Nerk*, and never to be confused with the properly long vowels of Delaware's *New-ark*.) Stephanie doesn't live in an idyllic little suburb, and she didn't work in one, either. In fact, her job was axed when E. E. Martin, the lingerie firm in question, was discovered to be connected to the mob. She wasn't working at Disneyworld, no indeed. Yet the humor is still there—Stephanie is, after all, a former lingerie buyer, a woman whose day revolved around thongs and lacy D-cups. Losing her job may suck, but it wasn't as if she was chained up in a sweatshop. And her particular brand of business expertise doesn't qualify her for much else other than a job doing the same thing—or working for her cousin Vinnie.

In Stephanie's world, late car payments mean exactly what it does in the real world—the threat of repossession and a battered, new-only-to-you Chevy Nova nearly too embarrassing to be seen in. In the real world, getting laid off can mean a string of thankless temp jobs that barely pay the rent, much less buy the groceries. There's usually no conveniently dead distant relative to leave you millions and a quaint house by the sea. There's almost never a charmingly perfect new career, serendipitously discovered through the magic of "one door closing and another opening." Yet, in the real world, most of us a) don't have a cousin Vinnie (or, if we do, most of the time he doesn't run a bail bonding operation), and b) would think twice before trading in those thankless temp jobs for mace, a gun, and the possibility of daily run-ins with criminals. The delicious irony here is how easy Stephanie makes it look (well, relatively anyway) and the fact that she actually succeeds. Tracing skips may not be easy, or a particularly glamorous job, but as Stephanie proves, even a former underwear buyer can do it.

What's most delicious about this contrast is Evanovich's portrayal of men like Ranger. Hard-ass, tough-as-nails guys who work a "man's job" and make no bones about the fact, at least at first, that a pretty little thing like Stephanie really has no business there. Of course, even Stephanie knows from the outset that screwing up *this* job will result in tougher consequences than her car's repossession and a few more shared pot-roasts with her parents than she'd like. Screwing up when you're tracking down someone charged with a felony could mean dying, which is pretty much the most unforgiving consequence anyone could face. I don't think Evanovich treats it lightly, but I do think she knows full well how charming it is to readers to find that Stephanie beats all the odds and succeeds at the end of every book. This is a woman who formerly worked a desk job, for heaven's sake. A woman who owns a *hamster*.

Stephanie's "unforgiving world" fits the noir checklist, albeit Evanovich's twisted version of it. Noir settings tend to be urban and gritty when they're not simply remote and kind of creepy. New Jersey's capital, Trenton ("Trenton Makes, the World Takes!" proclaims the sign over one of its bridges, referring to a manufacturing history long past it glory days) is also the Mercer County Seat. That means it's chock full of courthouses and government offices, as well as New Jersey State Prison, which houses the state's most violent offenders. This is definitely not a moneyed suburban enclave. But, true to form,

Evanovich has put a sideways spin on that merciless noir setting. If the grittier urban aspects of Trenton are the grimy nails, shifty eyes, and bullet-riddled limbs of the city, the Burg is its heart, always beating, a constant for Stephanie and so many others in the Plumverse.

That said, the Burg is invested in its own brand of unforgiving, if ripe for humor, censure. There, not only does everyone know everyone else's business, they talk about it, too—sometimes right to your face. In moneyed suburban enclaves everyone may know everyone else's business, but at least it's not up for block-wide discussion, unlike cousin Vinnie's sexual proclivities, for instance. Or take Mrs. Morelli's words to Stephanie in *One For the Money*: "Does your mother know you're carrying a gun? I'm going to tell her" (43). Even if its citizens' eccentricities aren't cause for good old-fashioned shunning, Stephanie's Trenton is not the soul of discretion, nor of politely looking the other way. You may not get kicked out of the Burg for wearing biker shorts past sixty, but it doesn't mean people aren't going to raise their eyebrows and make jokes.

Of course, it's absurd—and absurdly funny—that in the first book one of the people Stephanie is most apprehensive to face is the mother of the boy who took her virginity, not the boy himself—now a former cop charged with murder. And that's just another one of the ways Evanovich twists the noir tropes so beautifully. Grandma Mazur, Morelli himself, Ranger, Vinnie, and Lula, to name just a few, are representative of the kinds of characters noir employs so well, even if they've been recast here in surprising ways.

Noir uses iconic characters to shorthand plot twists and themes, just as other genres do, and the Plumverse is no exception. Stephanie herself is the most important example: the alienated protagonist. Alienation is a tricky concept; what makes someone alienated and not simply pissed off, or depressed, or otherwise anti-social? If you've alienated yourself from others purposely, does that count? I don't think there's a hard and fast definition that fits every situation, but for my purposes, alienation means that someone is simply set apart from his or her peer group in fundamental ways.

And Stephanie certainly fits the bill, at least on the surface. In a world that rewards success and money, Stephanie is clearly a failure. At the beginning of *One for the Money*, she's unemployed, divorced, and desperate—not the hallmarks of success in Trenton or anywhere else in the good old U.S. of A. Yet it's clear that Stephanie is better off without her deadbeat ex-husband, and that her previous job wasn't exactly a shining example of a career. Stephanie largely alienates herself from what other women her age are doing—or at least how they go about getting the things they want—and I think that's an important distinction. She may be pissed off about the Miata, but when push comes to shove, she's not going to wilt like a summer flower because she can't afford nail polish and Starbucks anymore.

Getting her Miata back doesn't work out, but even though it seems that skip tracing does, it doesn't make her any less alienated. How many women do you know who are bounty hunters, after all? Who choose carrying a gun and staking out FTAs to make a living instead of settling for a comfortable secretarial gig? Stephanie may be a couple of thousand dollars wealthier at the close of the first book in the series, but she's no closer to "fitting in" than she was at its start—but she may be a whole lot happier than women who do.

And isn't that what makes Stephanie so sympathetic to readers? It is for me. She doesn't settle for safe or sensible, and canny readers probably suspected it from her first mention of playing "choo-choo" in the Morellis' garage. Stephanie takes risks to get what she wants— even if, at the beginning, all she wants is some food in the fridge. Taking the job with Vinnie may not be a dream come true, but it's also not the end of the road the way the same sort of job would be for a classic noir protagonist.

Traditionally, of course, the alienated protagonist is a man, and that's one of the first tip-offs that this take on noir subverts the tropes. This twist is a big part of my love for Stephanie Plum. During noir's heyday, a man was the one to track down the killer, or stumble onto a mafia plot—or get his heart, and possibly his person, dragged through the mud and back by a *femme fatale*. The Plumverse, of course, features Stephanie in the leading role, which means Stephanie has *hommes fatales* to contend with.

That's right. Just as Stephanie turned the idea of the traditional male protagonist on its head, Morelli and Ranger are excellent substitutes for the seductive, dangerous women who so often appear in film noir. Mata Hari is probably the extreme of the *femme fatale*—the WWII-era spy who used her sexual allure to gather information from the enemy. Naturally, that's not the only way Evanovich plays with the character type. If anything of Stephanie's is in danger thanks to Morelli and Ranger, it's her hormones and her heart, which is what makes these particular *hommes* so endearing—at least to readers. *Femme fatale* translates literally as "fatal woman," but it's clear that their male counterparts in the Plumverse are nowhere near the same kind of threat.

Morelli's apparently been working his *homme fatale* vibe since childhood. Women aren't the only ones who use good looks to get what they want from the opposite sex (even if what they want is simply...well, sex). And Morelli knows how to use his, with Stephanie and most of Trenton's female population, if the rumors are true. He's a hometown boy turned vice cop, turned fugitive, turned vice cop once more, with enough connections to keep Stephanie abreast of skips' hideouts and Trenton gossip, and enough sex appeal for an entire police force.

And, yes, Stephanie falls for him. During choo-choo and later, in the bakery. But does she stand for his love 'em and leave 'em behavior? No way. She runs him over with her father's Buick, and when she meets up with him again in *One for the Money*, she makes sure to keep her distance—well, at first. Not only that, she spreads a rumor that he knocked her up! This is fantasy vengeance, a gorgeous little twist on the idea of a protagonist so vulnerable to sexual allure, he or she is ruined.

Ranger's just as tempting, and his mysterious background adds a whole other level of temptation to a package that's already hot, hard, and heavy on the you-know-you-want-me grins. And both Morelli and Ranger serve a purpose in the series. They usually have something Stephanie needs, whether it's information or advice or wheels. The fact that they each manage to pique her interest in activities that are definitely *not* job-related is a hazard she faces with varying degrees of aplomb. (And I don't blame her one bit.) And here's Evanovich holding up the trope to a funhouse mirror again—Stephanie is as dangerous to these two men as they are to her. As the series progresses, these tough guys fall hard for *her*.

That helps when Stephanie needs advice about tracking down skips (or figuring out what to do when she stumbles onto a corpse, or into a kidnapping plot, or any of the other outrageous situations in which she finds herself). In classic film noir, murder, crime, and corruption are usually part of the plot, and the movies feature characters to go with them. Stephanie's world is no different—look at what she does! Bail jumpers might not always be hardened criminals, but for the most part Stephanie's daily milieu is full of people even more desperate than she is. People with secrets, people with pasts, people who were arrested with lots and *lots* of reason. True in the Plumverse...or is it? Well, yes. No one would call Ramirez, or the variety of murderers, extortionists, and kidnappers featured in the series, a bumbling criminal, after all. But the Plumverse is an equal opportunity criminal milieu—they may not be entirely aboveboard, law-abiding citizens, but the irritable dwarf, the freaky Arabian sheik, and the pair of stoners who deal in stolen goods are a little more interesting than the garden-variety hardened criminals Stephanie has to track down. It's another absurdity that hits home surprisingly well. Sure, the dwarf is funny, but he's also *understandable*. Crime isn't only for the true psychos out there, Evanovich seems to be saying. It's not only not always a matter of life and death, it's sometimes, well...funny.

Which brings us to what's maybe the bedrock of noir, the issue of morality. Nine times out of ten, at least in classic noir, it's the lack of morality that defines a character or a plot point, and the Plumverse isn't very different. Some of it's a given, of course—a strong sense of ethics isn't high on the priority list for most criminals, or skips. But in Stephanie's world it's not just the bail-jumpers who twist their morals to suit their own needs. One of the first things Stephanie is told about Ranger is that he "doesn't always play by the rules" (*One for the Money* 33). And let's face it, in the first book, murder rap or not, Morelli jumping bail and hiding out until he can clear his name is probably not the police-approved method of facing criminal charges.

Are Stephanie's *hommes fatales* the only ones to view their morals as more of a loose guideline than a hard and fast code? Not by a long shot. Skip tracing by nature isn't exactly a playing-by-the-rules kind of job, and for that matter neither is private investigation or even police work (although the latter probably should be). In the first book alone, completely new to the job, Stephanie steals Morelli's car (well, she "commandeers" it) and lies, more than once. Not grievous errors on the scale of one to ten, but the fact that she's willing to do both so easily proves a) a probable predilection for her job, and b) that basic noir attitude of the ends justifying the means.

The difference is that we understand, and usually approve of, Stephanie's means and motives. Morelli may not deserve, in the strictest sense, the rumor that he knocked Stephanie up, but it provides a few envious moments of "I wish I could have done that" on the part of readers. Does Vinnie's initial refusal of a job for Stephanie warrant a threat of blackmail? When his sexual proclivities are that bizarre, come on—it's a given. I'm willing to give Stephanie the benefit of the doubt—I'm willing to bend my own rules of morality to see her succeed, because in the end she's trying to do something right, and she's not hurting anyone who hasn't bent the rules so many times they're accordion-pleated anyway. Unlike true noir, in which the protagonists, and others, sometimes "bend the rules" in ways that make us squirm with discomfort, Stephanie's reasons provide a kind of wish fulfillment.

Of course, Stephanie is the one who has to consider the ramifications of what she's doing and what kind of career she's embarked upon. Bounty hunting isn't for everyone, certainly, and it doesn't come with many easy outs when she's forced to make a choice about nailing a skip or waving good-bye to the bounty. In the end of *One for the Money*, for example, Stephanie's killed Jimmy Alpha in self-defense. She's a little bit regretful because she's taken a life, which is never something to take lightly, but she killed a man who was planning to offer her up to the questionable mercies of Benito Ramirez. Understandable, no doubt. The fact that she got shot in the ass for her trouble gives some ironic punctuation to the episode, in that "it might bite you in the ass later" sense. Stephanie's made a choice about being a bounty hunter, and the sheer absurdity that she's survived it doesn't mean her new job is going to be smooth sailing from here on out.

Noir was a reaction to world events that were unsympathetic in the extreme—Nazism, for one—and the inevitability of death was only one way to illustrate what many of the filmmakers felt was the futility of life. And that's where the Plumverse and film noir truly part ways, in my opinion. In noir, no one ends up truly happy—it's not possible in the world the characters inhabit. To quote Thomas Hobbes: "The life of man [is] solitary, poor, nasty, brutish, and short"—at least in film noir. That sums it up pretty cleanly for ill-fated characters such as Joe Gillis in *Sunset Boulevard* and Walter Neff in *Double Indemnity*.

Stephanie's world is far more hopeful than that. For one thing, catching the bad guys *does* ensure a degree of satisfaction, not just for Stephanie but for the citizens of Trenton. For every conspiracy, for every crime, for every scandal, there's a corresponding moment of hope, whether it's Grandma Mazur getting a new boyfriend (or her driver's license), or Lula joining the ranks of the gainfully employed, or Rex's improbable survival, or Stephanie's proposal of marriage from Morelli (and a proposal of something a little more sinful from Ranger). Stephanie's world may be unforgiving, but it's not hopeless. She's not doomed to sorrow and poverty and bad cars. (Okay, that last bit may be debatable.)

In the Plumverse, the noir attitude of cynicism and hopelessness is turned on its head. There's plenty of sarcasm in the book, but Stephanie isn't entirely jaded, and she's clearly hopeful about some degree of happiness in her life. What's more, the "grim realities" that are so often the meat and potatoes of noir are here transformed into cheese doodles and pigs in a blanket—odd, interesting, and very often funny. No one who can see the absurdity in getting shot in the ass is the kind of cynic you find in true noir. And part of Stephanie's lopsided optimism has to come from knowing that there will always be the Burg, there will always be pot-roast, and there will always be family. If the Plumverse is going truly to subvert any of the rules of noir, I'm certainly glad that it's this one.

AMY GARVEY is a former editor who now works on the other side of the desk as an author. Writing romance spiced with mystery gives her a chance to make up stories featuring dead people, hot sex, and humor, which seems like a pretty good way to make a living to her. Check out her Web site at www.amygarvey.com.

References

"Film Noir." *Wikipedia.* 18 June 2006. <http://en.wikipedia.org/wiki/Film_noir>

EXPLODING THE MYTH OF THE JERSEY GIRL

Devon Ellington

There are some things about Stephanie that are hard for the average non-Jersey girl to relate to: the excessive hairspray; the tight tops; the deep appreciation for spandex. But Stephanie's nerve? Her humor? Her longing for happiness and security? They're universal.

"EVERYTHING IN NEW JERSEY has a bad odor. It's one of the few things a person can count on" (38). That's one of Stephanie Plum's early comments in the first of her adventures, *One for the Money*. The first time I read those lines, I howled with laughter. I've spent many an hour on the New Jersey highways, windows rolled up, holding my nose as I drove past Newark or "The Toxic Swamp" around the Meadowlands. And just recently, in January 2007, frantic 911 calls were made from Washington Heights to Greenwich Village about a noxious, gas-like odor. Midtown office buildings were evacuated, and the PATH train was shut down for two hours. No one, including Con Edison or the Emergency Services/Terrorist Task Force teams, could figure out immediately what it was—but it was believed to be wafting over the Hudson River from Jersey. You read Stephanie's words and you laugh; they're funny, but they're also true. There's a dryness, a wryness, in the line, and it's one of the hints that Evanovich is not going to use Stephanie to embody a cliché, but explode it.

Every culture has its myths, be it fourth century B.C. Etruscans or twenty-first century A.D. Americans. When we think of Greek, Roman, and Celtic myths, we think of pantheons of gods and goddesses, and stories that explain the behavior of the natural world. Today, the word is often used just to refer to something—say, a popular story or belief—that isn't true. Focusing on the myth as something that is false makes it easy to forget that, false though they may be, all myths are, at heart, stories meant to explain things: why the sun comes up in the morning—or why girls with Jersey accents always have such big hair.

The myth of the Jersey girl explains who these particular girls are and what they want; it's a form of shorthand that lets viewers and readers achieve a basic understanding of a particular character quickly. And there's certainly some truth to the myth; there would have to be, or we wouldn't see it so often. But we've seen the Jersey girl so often that she's become a cliché. What Evanovich has done so successfully is redeem the cliché, turning the Jersey girl from someone we think we know (and can therefore dismiss) into a real person, whom we can care about and sympathize with. Evanovich isn't content just to repeat the myth. Instead she takes us beyond it to create a real character on a real journey. That's why her audience has stayed with her for twelve (to date) Stephanie Plum books (plus holiday specials), created a market for her pre-Plum romance novels' re-issuance, and gobbled up her new series starring Baltimore-raised mechanic extraordinaire Alexandra Barnaby as quickly as Evanovich has been able to write them.

The early books take us into the familiar Jersey myth. Although in each book, Stephanie moves beyond expectations to show she's more than a mere cipher, the early books set up the solid foundation she needs in order to soar in the later ones. In *One for the Money*, she is well suited to epitomize the Jersey Girl cliché, joining the ranks of Marisa Tomei's character Mona Lisa Vito in *My Cousin Vinny*, the women of *The Sopranos*, and characters from innumerable forgettable television sitcoms. She wears spandex and acts like a hockey jersey is the height of fashion. She carries hairspray in her purse to preserve the big, Jersey hair (Jersey girls can rival Texas girls when it comes to big hair). She has the red lipstick. She firmly believes that, when in doubt, add mascara. She used to be a lingerie buyer for a discount store. She knows how to remove a distributor cap from a car. And she's not alone. Her friend Mary Lou fits the stereotype, as does the office manager of her cousin Vinnie's bail bonds office, Connie. They have the big hair; they're man-hungry; they're loud; and they dress in tight clothes.

They're women we recognize and are prepared to laugh at. They're the ones we make fun of when we go out. They're noisy and crude, not at all "like us." We go out with our female friends and don't worry about not having a date on a Friday night. We don't think wearing a size too small makes a top or a pair of jeans sexy. We're career women who'll get married when *we* want to, not when someone else "from the neighborhood" thinks we should. We're more sophisticated, educated, and self-confident. So what if we have a few too many drinks at the bar with our girlfriends on Friday nights and get a little loud? At least we're not from *Jersey*.

The second book, *Two for the Dough*, pokes even more fun at Jersey stereotypes. In the beauty parlor, Stephanie runs into her nemesis, Joyce Barnhardt (the woman with whom Stephanie caught her husband fornicating on their brand new dining room table), and the two *women* (in true *male* fashion) compare gun sizes (they're phallic symbols after all). Immediately, every other female in the shop pulls out a gun and starts discussing the pros and cons of their preferred (and proffered) weapon. Move over boys; these Jersey girls are not to be trifled with!

Evanovich uses the idea of Jersey girls as bossy and desperate and takes it a clever step further, pushing the envelope but in familiar territory. Almost despite ourselves, we start to respect these self-sufficient women. We're still laughing, but the tone changed. There's something admirable about a group of women tough enough to carry loaded weapons in their purses instead of expecting to be rescued by some guy. We weren't expecting this type of self-sufficiency. Now we're intrigued. Maybe there's more to these Jersey girls than we originally thought.

In the third book, *Three to Get Deadly*, Stephanie explains the resilience of Jersey residents: "Adaptation is one of the great advantages to being born and bred in Jersey. We're simply not bested by bad air or tainted water. We're like that catfish with lungs. Take us out of our environment and we can grow whatever body parts we need to survive. After Jersey the rest of the country's a piece of cake. You want to send someone into a fallout zone? Get him from Jersey. He'll be fine" (523). Maybe having someone from Jersey around *isn't* such a bad idea.

One or two such references are dropped into book after book—because Jersey girls are *proud* to be Jersey girls. They're *proud* to be loud and *proud* of the disdain shown by non-Jersey girls. You don't want to be friends with me? To hell with you! I got real friends—in Jersey! Jersey girls make noise. They demand attention. In December 2006, a group of Trenton hookers stood in protest on the side of the road, in full spandex and tight V-neck shirts, cigarettes dangling out of their mouths. No one knew what the protest was about—but they got massive media attention in the tri-state region. They got noticed.

As the books progress, we're no longer laughing *at* these women, we're laughing *with* them. When Maxine Nowicki gets away with a million dollars in *Four to Score*, after tricking her abusive ex into confessing about his counterfeiting scheme and tattooing him head-to-toe with messages like "pencil dick" and "woman beater," we're rooting for her. We want Maxine, her mother, and Margie to get away and start a new life. We're rooting for Evelyn in *Hard Eight* when her daughter Annie takes the vicious Abruzzi's Napoleon medal by mistake, and Evelyn realizes it's her ticket out of a life of poverty and abuse. These women may be down and out, but they're resourceful. They don't play it safe. They take risks.

Stephanie, in a pretty risky business herself, admires those risks. Women like Maxine and Evelyn get another chance at life thanks to Stephanie and the choices she makes when faced with their stories. She doesn't respond to them the way Ranger, or Dog of television bounty-hunting fame, would. She sees these women as individuals and treats them with compassion, respect, and, most importantly, dignity—and because we live the Plum stories through Stephanie's eyes, we experience these women the same way. There's humor—Maxine's tattoo revenge—but there's also pathos. These are real people, with real tragedies, beneath the comedy.

Stephanie herself is the first Jersey girl we learn to respect, and the one we end up relating to well enough to follow her through twelve-plus adventures. When Stephanie steals Morelli's distributor cap in *One for the Money*, we expect, in true, loud, Jersey girl fashion, that she will wave it under his nose. She doesn't; she hides it under a bush so she can retrieve it at will. She's smart enough to look at the big picture, not just for a quick adrenaline shot of revenge. She's resourceful and that's a quality we admire. We'd like to think we would be as clever in a similar situation.

When Emanuel Lowe tells Stephanie he'll obey her command to lie down on the floor "if you show me some pussy. It's got to be good pussy, too. The full show...." Stephanie doesn't bother to respond with a verbal retort. She shoots him in the little toe. "I did it for women worldwide," she explains afterward. "It was a public service" (*Eleven on Top* 83). Every women who's ever been hassled by a nasty twerp of a guy stands up and cheers at that point. And at the moment we do so, living vicariously through Stephanie as she does what we wish we could have or would have done in the same situation, she stops being a cliché, someone *over there*. The experience is more than understanding someone with a different frame of reference— in that moment, we are united. And so, when we start to encounter other wounded yet resilient and resourceful Jersey women through Stephanie's experience, we start to change our preconceptions. By living through Stephanie, we become more open-minded.

But let's step back for a minute and look more closely at Stephanie, and how Evanovich gives our familiar Jersey girl such unexpected depth. Evanovich has said of Stephanie, "We're both from Jersey and we both graduated from Douglass College. . . I wouldn't go so far as to say Stephanie is a completely autobiographical character, but I will admit to knowing where she lives" (*How I Write* 10–11). Who better than a Jersey girl to help us get inside another one's head. Or to remind us that, like any stereotype, the myth of the Jersey girl only describes a general pattern of behavior, it doesn't tell us about individual people or the reality of their lives?

Jersey accents are well-documented in television and movies. To an untrained ear, a Jersey accent sounds the same as a Brooklyn, Bronx, Queens, Staten Island, or even Long Island cadence, but to people who live in the area and hear the different inflections every day, it's a different story. Professor Henry Higgins of *My Fair Lady* might boast that he can narrow down the street where any Londoner lives by the way the person speaks, but a New Yorker's going to be able to tell you more than the borough of the speaker, he'll tell you the neighborhood. A London Cockney might drop his "g's," but a guy from Long Island will drag that "g" over into the next word, especially if it begins with a vowel. Someone from Jersey (be it Newark, Atlantic City, or Trenton) is going to speak with a combination of nasal and low chest inflections, with plenty of upper-register whine. Their laugh will tend to be a short, braying spurt.

We don't actually hear Stephanie speak, of course, but we do get a sense of her speech pattern, and it's one of the first signs that Stephanie will not be merely a cliché despite the hair and the biker shorts. Cadence defines character. If a character speaks in a particular rhythm, the reader will make assumptions about the character's background, economic status, education status, and, often, intelligence. But open a Plum novel to any page and read a few paragraphs: Stephanie sounds like what she is—a college-educated woman. She's going to respond to a nasty comment with a smart-ass one of her own when appropriate, but it's going to be something a lot more interesting than "Up yours." When she goes to Virginia to help question Carmen Cruz's friends and family in *Twelve Sharp* and introduces herself as part of the task force, no one questions it. She's well-spoken enough that she is able to pass as a local investigator rather than being immediately marked as a Jersey girl. When she travels to Vegas in search of Samuel Singh in *To the Nines*, Connie and Lula are screaming Jersey advertisements, but Stephanie can fit in anywhere—which is different than her claim in earlier books that a Jersey-ite can *adapt* anywhere. Stephanie doesn't just adapt, she fits. Anywhere except within the confines of her own hometown, that is, where at her age she is supposed to be married and popping out babies.

In the Burg, Stephanie just doesn't quite fit the mold. Her friend Mary Lou fits it perfectly—Mary Lou married young, complains about her husband and her life, but would rather stay in a frustrating marriage than try to make it on her own. When I was growing up in Westchester, the boys constantly joked that if they wanted to get laid, they'd go into the city and find a Jersey girl because Jersey girls will sleep with anyone rather than spend the night alone. However, few Westchester boys would bring a Jersey girl home—they were girls for a good time, not girls to marry or even acknowledge as girlfriends. And the stereotypical Jersey girl is desperate to marry. She might hunt a Westchester boy or a Manhattan boy or a Long Island boy, but chances are she'll marry someone from the Burg—someone she grew up with. And stick with him, no matter how badly he treats her. The typical Jersey girl would rather have a cheating husband than no husband.

Stephanie tried marriage, as was expected of her. But when she walked in on her husband cheating with Joyce Barnhardt on her and husband Dickie's new dining room table, she didn't put up with it.

She divorced him—which is against Jersey stereotype. Jersey girls get left—they don't do the leaving. Stephanie steps out of that prison.

Child-bearing is another minefield Stephanie's managed to avoid, in spite of her heritage. Plenty of Jersey girls who try to trap, or keep, their man by having a baby end up as single mothers in the end. Even Stephanie's sister Valerie, the Jersey girl who tried to transform herself into a golden California cupcake, is left by her husband with two children to raise. By avoiding the baby trap, Stephanie also keeps herself from falling prey to another more sobering Jersey stereotype, one that Jon Katz so beautifully portrays in his Jersey-based Kit Deleeuw novels, especially *Death by Station Wagon*. Parts of Jersey are filled with women, he observes, who spend their early twenties on the career fast-track, then marry and move to the suburbs, where it's "safe." They focus on their role as stay-at-home mom with the same ferocity they used to use in climbing the career ladder—and get lost. They find their stay-at-home lives unsatisfying but can't force themselves back to work, and they're terrified that letting their kids out of sight for even a moment means they're no longer necessary—if their children don't need them, they have nothing. Deleeuw calls them "The Lost Women."

These women are either college-educated Jersey girls (similar to Stephanie) or Manhattan- or Westchester-raised girls with careers in the city who moved out to the more affordable Jersey with their husbands and fell into the traditional roles of the 1950s housewife. Had Stephanie packed up and moved east to the big, bad city of Manhattan to make her fortune, she might have become trapped in this myth as well.

Without the expectations of these myths and stereotypes to guide her, however, even Stephanie's not quite sure where she's heading. The Jersey girl plays hard when she's young, but always with an eye on the Man She's Gonna Marry. And then, the babies she's going to have. And then...well, few think that far ahead, and by the time they get there, they're worn out. It isn't until they get to be Grandma Mazur's age, and, preferably, are widowed, that they get to have fun again and be individuals. For Stephanie, marriage was a tangent that didn't work out. She's in Jersey—her options are limited. She doesn't want to end up working at the tampon factory. And she's too tied to her family, emotionally, to do more than travel with Ranger on a job or go to Vegas after a skip. While television portrayals of Jersey tend to focus on Newark, only a PATH ride away from the bright lights of Manhattan, Stephanie's in Trenton, close to the Pennsylvania border. She's probably not going to find her heart's desire in Amish country. Hairspray and mascara are forbidden there, and, no matter how far she's willing to stretch the stereotype, there are some things about being a Jersey girl she will *not* give up. For Stephanie, the mascara wand is more powerful than the gun. It gives her a sense of security the gun can't. And she remembers to put the mascara in her purse, whereas the gun tends to stay home.

Stephanie comes to bounty hunting because she needs a job; by *Eleven on Top*, she's decided to quit the bounty hunting game, tired of being chased, shot at, slimed, and flashed. She's on a quest for another way to make a living—because maybe when she finds her professional calling, her life will make sense. So she tries—at the button factory, at Kan Klean Dry Cleaners, at Cluck in a Bucket. If she were simply out to pay the bills long enough to snag another husband, the way a Jersey girl should be, these dreadful jobs in horrible environments wouldn't faze her—but she's not. At this point in her life, she's finding out more about what she doesn't want than what she does, and, although she knows her family loves her deeply, she also knows they don't understand her. And that feeling makes her strive harder. At least dealing with FTAs gives her a focus. Lula gives her unconditional friendship. And Joe and Ranger give her love, on terms with which they can all deal, for the moment at least, separate from their Jersey society's demands. And that's where Evanovich most succeeds in exploding the myth of the Jersey girl—no matter how we stereotype Stephanie going in, that searching is something we can all relate to.

Evanovich sums up her writing goals in several passages of her book *How I Write*:

> Being a writer also gives me the opportunity to make people happy, so I write positive books. When a reader is done with one of my books, I want him to feel good. I want him to like his kids better. I want him to like the dog. I want him to feel really good about himself, like he could accomplish something. Maybe his life isn't turning out the way he thought it would, but that doesn't mean it doesn't have value (186)....I think my books make people hap-

py, and that's my principal appeal. My characters (sometimes even the bad guys) are positive, likeable people who are incredibly average, and yet they can be heroic if necessary. They make people laugh and feel good about themselves. If Stephanie Plum can make it through the day, so can my reader (40)....So, Stephanie will forever be thirty, Ranger will always be sexy, and Rex the hamster will never die (35).

Now *there's* a myth worth living.

DEVON ELLINGTON publishes under a half a dozen names in both fiction and non-fiction. Her work appears in publications including *Wild Child*, *Rose and Thorn*, *Hampton Family Life*, *Emerging Women Writers*, *Femmefan*, and *Toasted Cheese*. Her plays are produced in New York, Los Angeles, London, Edinburgh, and Australia. For two years, she wrote four serials in four genres—mystery, western, magical realism, and action/adventure/pirate—for *Keep It Coming*. She writes the Literary Athlete column for *The Scruffy Dog Review*, her Web site is www.devonellingtonwork.com, and her blog on the writing life is "Ink in My Coffee" (devonellington. wordpress.com).

References

Evanovich, Janet with Ina Yalof. *How I Write: Secrets of a Bestselling Author*. New York: St. Martin's Griffin, 2006.

Katz, Jon. *Death by Station Wagon*. New York: Bantam, 1994.

Malory, Sir Thomas. *Le Morte D'Arthur*. New York: Modern Library New Edition, 1999.

LEARNING TO FLY

WHY BOUNTY HUNTING IS MORE THERAPEUTIC THAN RUNNING OVER MORELLI WITH A BUICK

Sylvia Day

When we first meet Stephanie, she can't afford therapy—she can barely afford her low-rent apartment and regular meals. A couple of hours a week with a trained professional, not that you'd have talked her into it, probably would have done her good. Luckily, as Sylvia Day suggests, she found bounty hunting instead.

> Bounty hunter. It held a certain cachet.
>
> —Stephanie Plum, *Three to Get Deadly* (3)

This simple statement is Stephanie Plum in a nutshell. But it is important to note that while the statement itself is simple, the reasons why such a thing would be important to Stephanie are a little more complicated.

Yes, superficially, the job carries a certain prestige that Steph finds appealing. When Janet Evanovich first introduces us to our intrepid heroine, it's only a few days before Stephanie pursues her first bounty. But as her story unfolds and we hear more about her past, our picture of her broadens. We learn that, as a child, she was stifled and misunderstood in a dysfunctional family in which she felt like an outsider. Her mother is Trenton's second answer to *Desperate Housewives*'s Bree Van De Kamp (after Mrs. Morelli, who is said to make all other Burg housewives look second-rate), her father is negligent in his duty to provide a strong father figure, and her older sister Valerie is (or at least was, before her husband left her) perfect in every way, setting an example Stephanie could never live up to. Steph spent her early years feeling insignificant, and went on to a forgettable stint at Douglass

College and a lamentable marriage to an unworthy man she never seemed to be very attached to. When asked why she married Dickie Orr, she replies it was because he had a nice car. Translation: She has no idea.

Stephanie made these choices knowing they were the wrong ones for her. They were, however, the choices her family (most likely her mother) approved of.

I

Two blocks to my parents' house, and I could feel familial obligation sucking at me, pulling me into the heart of the Burg. The clock on the dash told me I was seven minutes late, and the urge to scream told me I was home.

—Stephanie Plum, *One for the Money* (7)

Prior to Stephanie stumbling into bounty hunting, the impetus for most of her decisions was fulfilling familial expectations. Going to college and marrying a lawyer were never goals she had set for herself.

Stephanie was a square peg trying to fit into the rounded hole of a housewife that Valerie filled so beautifully, and Steph's failure left her as the odd child out. For Mrs. Plum, the roles of wife and mother constitute her entire identity. They define her world, and she seems capable of relating to her daughters only when they live inside these roles, too. This is partly why Mrs. Plum is constantly suggesting jobs more worthy of a high school student than a woman in her early thirties: in her mind, Stephanie should be holding a job that can be easily discarded when she marries and assumes her true career as a housewife. When we first meet Steph, her mother laments her clothes as being a deterrent to men, then goes on to list potential boyfriends without using any type of criterion for selection. If they're male, they are a possible husband.

These machinations, while driven by the best of intentions, reinforce to Stephanie that she can't be trusted to make important decisions on her own. The poor quality of the men her mother suggests is insulting, clearly expressing Mrs. Plum's belief that Steph should gratefully take what she can get. Is it any wonder that a career with a "certain cachet" would be so appealing? Being a bounty hunter undeniably elevates Stephanie to above-average.

Yes, she's an ordinary girl, living an ordinary life, but she dreams of the extraordinary. Her role model isn't her mother. It's Wonder Woman.

> Not only did Wonder Woman spill over her Wondercups but she also kicked serious ass. If I had to name the single most influential person in my life it would have to be Wonder Woman.
>
> —Stephanie Plum, *Three to Get Deadly* (166)

Her role model is a superheroine—a perfect mix of abundant femininity, physical power, and innate confidence that commands respect. In today's world, the closest a gal can get to this ideal is as a bounty hunter. Unlike if she were in the military or police force, Stephanie gets to make up her own rules as she goes along. For Steph, the illusion of control that comes with the title "bounty hunter" is a powerful lure. She may not overfill Wondercups, but she can track down skips.

II

> Morelli: You were nuts. You'd do anything. You used to jump off your father's garage, trying to fly.
> Stephanie: Didn't you ever try to fly?
> Morelli: No. Never. I knew I couldn't fly.
>
> —*Three to Get Deadly* (302)

Steph isn't mentally challenged. She manages to land in more scrapes than most, but she's an intelligent gal. She knows she can't fly. So why do something that seems so "nuts," as Morelli says? We can't write it off as youthful fancy, and it's not something she did purely for the excitement of trying it. Stephanie is too complicated to give so simple an answer. For her, trying to fly is a physical manifestation of her desperate desire to be *more* than what the world sees when it looks at her.

I might be a stay-at-home mother someday, but I'll always be trying to fly off the garage roof. That's just who I am.

—Stephanie Plum, *Seven Up* (304)

With all of this baggage, you can see why a job with no set hours, a hint of danger, the challenge of outwitting clever criminals, and lots of doughnuts would seem like a decent rest stop on the road to finding herself. It's about as far removed from her mother's life as Steph can get.

III

So let's talk about Joe. (Sigh.)

That Joe Morelli is Stephanie's first quarry is important to note, because catching him is the reason she sticks with bounty hunting instead of looking for something else once her immediate need for cash is met. She is desperate for money when she blackmails Vinnie into giving her the job, but when she gets her percentage of Joe's bond, she doesn't rush out and spend it right away. Ten grand may not stretch too far when you need to buy a car, too, but spent wisely, it could hold you through a few months while you are job hunting. She could have quit while she was ahead.

So what turns the temporary gig into a full-time job? The sense of accomplishment Stephanie gets first from collaring Joe and then from saving him by finding the proof of his innocence. But would it have been the same with another skip? I don't think so.

Their history makes catching Joe an irresistible challenge. His primary appeal to a youthful Stephanie was his bad reputation. Warning Steph away from anything is like waving a red cape before a raging bull. If she's told she can't do something, she has to prove the gainsayer wrong. In Joe's case, the entire Burg warned her away from him—and his father's garage.

[L]et's be truthful, you were hardly tricked. You practically knocked me over trying to get to the garage.

—Joe Morelli, *Three to Get Deadly* (303)

Later, when Morelli walked out of the Tasty Pastry and didn't look back (other than in poems written in the bathroom of Mario's Sub Shop and the stadium wall), his dismissal hurt Steph pretty badly. For a young girl already struggling with a dysfunctional family who couldn't fully appreciate her, being discarded and forgotten after giving up her virginity would have been crushing. Running Joe over with the Buick wasn't just about retribution. It was about forcing him to *see* her, to acknowledge her. Joe might not have remembered going at it behind the éclair case, but he sure as hell remembered getting run over.

So when Vinnie hires her on as a bounty hunter and gives her Joe's file, Stephanie's heart flips and she can't resist. Yes, the money is the main motivator . . . until she sees him again. His cocky getaway from the State Street apartment rouses her stubborn streak, except in this case she also has a grudge that has been only marginally satisfied by the Buick incident. Plus he's tough to track, and the more people who tell her she can't catch him, the more determined she becomes.

Had she started out with any other skip, things might have turned out differently. As it was, working *against* Morelli and then *with* him as she deals with both Ramirez and the erroneous charge against Joe builds Steph's confidence. Suddenly, her previously aimless days are filled with both physical and intellectual challenges, and the man who once used and discarded her is starting to respect her, even turn to her for help. That's a lot to expect from a job, but that's exactly what Stephanie gets, and quickly, from something that was only intended to tide her over until she found other employment.

IV

After Stephanie's first run in with Morelli, she goes home to regroup. When she hits the pavement again, she's dressed to impress in a beige linen suit, pantyhose, and heels. In her old life, this was the type of outfit that inspired the confidence she lacked. She wasn't happy with who she was, so she used her active imagination to picture herself as someone else. One of those fantasies was "an elegantly dressed woman, barking orders at toadying men while her limo waited at curbside" (*Three to Get Deadly* 166).

But Steph's self-confidence begins to grow, in large part due to her work as a bounty hunter. Yes, casual clothes make doing her job easier, but her ability to wear those clothes with aplomb comes from inside. She develops a healthy attitude toward her appearance, seeing it not as something her worth is judged on, but as the wrapping on a more confident package—a package worth a great deal more for its contents.

Stephanie starts out her bounty hunting career, with a trip to see Ramirez, in that linen suit, but she quickly finds out that what she wears isn't going to give her the strength she needs. In later books, she approaches skips more confidently *in spite* of what she's wearing, not *because* of it.

> Morelli had been watching me. "What happened to your hair?" he asked.
> "It's under my hat."
> He had his hands shoved into his jeans pockets. "Very sexy."
> —*Two for the Dough* (5)

It's not the hat-hair that catches Joe's eye, but the fact that she wears it so well. Stephanie slowly comes to realize that she's no longer invisible. She attracts the romantic attentions of two men who weren't able to see beyond her exterior prior to her blossoming. It's not *just* her appearance that counts.

V

> I tried to run at least three times a week. It never ever occurred to me I might enjoy it. I ran to burn off the occasional bottle of beer, and because it was good to be able to outrun the bad guys.
> —Stephanie Plum, *Two for the Dough* (36)

In *One for the Money*, Steph begins to get in shape after one too many crazed calls from Martinez. She continues her running regimen until the middle of *Three to Get Deadly*—at which point she discards the effort. She blames quitting on blisters. Truth is, she's becoming more aware of who she is, seeing her limitations and becoming more comfortable with them. Her focus alters from fitting another mold—that of bounty hunter—to taking on the job in her own way.

VI

A soft under-swell of reader complaints about Stephanie suggest that she's not growing as a bounty hunter. She has never become comfortable with carrying a gun, her apartment is broken into with alarming frequency, she's not moving up the hierarchy in Vinnie's company, and she's still kidnapped quite often. All good arguments, if the growth one seeks to find is in the career field itself. Thing is, being a bounty hunter has never been about the job for Steph. She starts out needing the money, but that quickly changes; it becomes a personal goal in response to Morelli, who continues to one-up her, and to the threat presented by Ramirez, which shakes her out of her complacency. She stays with the job, though, because it gives her a uniqueness that she always knew she had, even if no one else did. As her relationship with Morelli grows, the cases they work on give them a shared interest where before there was physical attraction between them but not much in the way of conversation. It is the strength they both discover in her through her job-related experiences that allows the relationship to progress from casual sex to love.

Presently, I think she hangs on to the job in part because it acts as a barrier to the role Morelli wishes her to assume—housewife. (Truly, I don't think he'd be completely happy with a Stephanie like that, but that's the topic of another essay altogether.) She also keeps the job because bond enforcement creates a tether to Ranger, a man who has always appreciated Stephanie for who she is and, no matter what, never tried to keep her from doing something she has wanted to do. Everyone else in her life attempts to discourage her, usually because they don't feel that she can handle the challenge. Ranger may only be humoring her, but by doing so, and acting as her safety net, he enables her to explore.

Stephanie has proven herself to be remarkably tenacious. It stands to reason that she could become an excellent, by-the-rules-book bounty hunter—if she really wanted to. In *One for the Money*, she hits the shooting range and becomes a crack shot in a very short amount of time, because she sets her mind to it. When she wants to find Kenny Mancuso, she camps out in the Buick despite cold, hunger, and fear. If she wanted to be a great bond enforcer, she would be one. Instead, she's assumed the role in her way, on her terms, and she's using the experience to find herself, to step away from her identity as a daughter and a divorcée and become a person in her own right.

A woman who jumped off the garage roof and proved that she can fly.

SYLVIA DAY is a former Russian linguist with the U.S. Army Military Intelligence. She sold her first novel thirteen months after she began writing and followed that with the sale of ten more within the next year to multiple publishers, including HarperCollins and Kensington. Her award-winning books have been called "wonderful and passionate" by WNBC.com, "wickedly entertaining" by *Booklist*, and frequently garner Readers' Choice and Reviewers' Choice accolades. She is a devout Morelli fan (while secretly carrying a torch for Ranger). Visit her at www.SylviaDay.com.

I LOVE STEPHIE

Carole Nelson Douglas

Bree, Lynette, Gabrielle, and Susan, Stephanie is not. (Well, maybe Susan—being locked out of your house naked is just the sort of situation Stephanie would be able to empathize with.) But she does have a lot in common with a zany, lovable Desperate Housewife of an earlier age: Lucy Ricardo.

WHAT IS IT ABOUT Janet Evanovich's Stephanie Plum series that has put her at the top of the *New York Times* bestseller list and made her loyal readers see purple? What has made them, in the words of Janet's promotional catch phrase, go "Plum Crazy" for thirteen laugh-a-lot years?

Is it Janet's unique mix of a quirky, loveable heroine with a quirky, lovable, but dysfunctional family? Is it the sinister-humorous take on East Coast Family in terms of the mob? Is it the dark underside of the humor: real danger and a slew of *Fargo*-like venal, bumbling psychopaths for Stephanie to go up against? Or the classic romantic triangle with two desirable Alpha guys courting a feisty gal trying to make it in a man's world just to pay the rent and keep her independence?

Or is it the inspired underpinnings of another comic leading lady from long ago and far away?

Janet told me once that she knew from the beginning that the series had to run on "the humor and the chase." That phrase could describe everything from *Keystone Kops* shorts in silent films to *Romancing the Stone*. The chase in this case is both criminal and romantic. The motive is Stephanie "getting her man." Criminal or criminally attractive. And the method in both pursuits is often hilariously comic.

Stephanie's Literally Comic Roots Are Showing

Janet has often cited an Uncle Scrooge comic book addiction as a child. (I had that one too.) So what was the Scrooge McDuck mystique? Well, he was literally rolling in money, yet his image—spats, top hat, cane, and reading specs—was smiling and lovable. And his adventures were imaginative and far-ranging—just like Stephanie Plum's.

Janet is so Uncle Scrooge-happy that, where other authors might name *Moby Dick* or *To Kill a Mockingbird* as the book that had the most significant impact on her life, she cites the Uncle Scrooge adventures by Carl Banks.

With such literally comic roots, no wonder humor is the hallmark of Janet's wildly successful mystery series: Stephanie's constantly exploding cars, the scatological dog-poop pranks, and the physical low comedy of some of Stephanie's "captures."

Take the window-mooning, self-exposing, oiled, and naked obese man in *To the Nines* who is too big, slippery, and obscene to submit to physical capture. Please take him. Stephanie can't. Not only that, what he is waving around only proves him insufficiently endowed.

Stephanie's clothes end up covered in Vaseline, and she's the object of racy comments for some time afterward. It's a literally dirty job, but somebody has to do it. Stephanie Plum does it to keep from giving up and giving in and moving back home, where we know she would become a desperately bored housewife.

It's easy to visualize Stephanie Plum, while in pursuit of an FTA, getting into a grape-stomping, no-holds-barred wrestling war with a hefty Italian woman who could be the Godfather in drag, or going undercover with Lula on a candy-box-stuffing assembly line...and then falling so behind that they start stuffing missed chocolate creams into their faces to hide the evidence...until their clothes, hair, and faces are smeared with feces-dark chocolate, making them look like guilty toddlers who got toilet training very, very wrong.

Those grape-stomping and chocolate-stuffing scenes are classic clips from the *I Love Lucy* show. It's humor at its most domestic and messiest, distaff humor that isn't afraid to get down-and-dirty physical and well as outrageous.

Maybe some readers find the Plum series humor raucous and vulgar, or some of the shtick (exploding dog poop dumped on mean girls' doorsteps) juvenile and rowdy, but so is the Burg, that earthy part of Trenton, New Jersey, that is Stephanie's beloved beat. Irreverence is the ethanol that makes cheeky comedy run, and Janet has that quality in spades, clubs, and hearts too.

The slapstick elements of the Plum series add up to a modern Three Stooges for Women, and that's no mean achievement. Even women who find the antics of Larry, Curly, and Moe a distinctly masculine taste realize that Stephanie Plum on a rowdy, rollicking roll is like Lucy on a rampage. You gotta laugh with this never-say-die dame.

Because the one entertainment icon who best embodies the heart and soul of Plumdom is Lucille Ball's Lucy Ricardo. There's a lot of Lucy in Stephanie Plum and her sometimes slapstick crime-solving and romantic antics.

Why We Have a Lucy to Love

In the early fifties, the still-new television was considered a lesser medium than film, but devalued aging actresses flocked to it: Ann Sothern, Loretta Young, and Ida Lupino. Lucille Ball did it first.

The other women played solely on their attractiveness and acting ability. Lucille Ball was the first gorgeous Hollywood actress to set herself up for outrageous, "undignified" physical comedy. The screwball comedies of the 1930s did allow some glamorous stars to cut loose: Carole Lombard and Katharine Hepburn spring to mind. But Lucille Ball imported that tradition to early television in the fifties, and took it up a notch. The actress had appeared in a raft of B-plus films without breaking out, but *I Love Lucy* made Lucille Ball a household name, a comic legend, and a woman mogul in the male-dominated screen industry. Her Desilu production company established both what TV could be and would become.

Desperate Housewives

I Love Lucy debuted in 1951, when America was busy getting Rosie the Riveter off the assembly lines to make room in the factories for returning GIs. Rosie, in her head kerchief and oil-spattered (*not* Vaseline-smeared) coveralls, was pushed aside, and America's women were ushered into the full-skirted super-femininity of the 1950s and love affairs with Frigidaires and vacuum cleaners.

Ball guarded her star image by contractually insisting sidekick Vivian Vance, as Ethel Mertz, dye her hair gray and eschew make-up. (The story that Vance was contractually obligated to remain twenty pounds heavier than Ball is an urban legend.) Yet Ball, after cannily protecting her silver screen beauty history, then proceeded to rubber-face her way through some all-time classic physical comedy routines. These were balanced by the "star turns" when Lucy would sneak into song-and-dance routines with TV husband Ricky Ricardo and his band.

The *I Love Lucy* show moved her Cuban bandleader husband, Desi Arnaz, into a role that made him one of the best "straight men" in the business. Few today can understand how hard it was to get a "mixed" marriage like Lucy and Desi's on early fifties TV. Ball and Arnaz had to take a song-and-dance act on the road to prove to the network that audiences would accept them as a couple in a TV series. They got rave reviews.

Despite the network's leeriness of a Latino husband with a pronounced Spanish accent, *I Love Lucy* scripts openly played up the hot-tempered Cuban angle as part of the comedy, and by doing so struck a blow for multiculturism. Also, Ricky's macho insistence on having a traditional wife, a housewife, didn't hurt at a time when the country wanted women at home consuming rather than out competing with men for jobs. And Lucy's dreams of stage stardom were suitably "fantastic." She wasn't a threatening fifties career woman, as portrayed in the Spencer Tracy/Katharine Hepburn proto-feminist films written by Garson Kanin and his wife, actress Ruth Gordon. Lucy was just a daffy post-war housewife with too much time on her hands, who laughably bungled all her hare-brained ambitions of working outside the home.

Almost all of Lucy Ricardo's adventures stem from her perpetual schemes to "get into show business" like her bandleader husband, Ricky. What plays like a ditzy housewife wanting attention and to be a star is really the saga of a woman needing a job outside the home, as Lucille Ball herself desperately needed a job outside of Hollywood films at that fortyish mid-point in her career.

In Janet's books, former lingerie saleswoman (hyping the superfeminine) Stephanie Plum crashes the "butch" criminal apprehension game as a bounty hunter. Lucy seeks to banish fifties housewife boredom. Steph just needs some dough to survive and has only family to depend on: the classically Joe Pesci-like "cousin Vinnie," a creepy bail bondsman who hands Stephanie low-end apprehension jobs. Like Lucy's constant schemes to get out of the house, these simple assignments escalate into comedies of errors, or sometimes, in Stephanie's case, comedies of terrors.

For underneath the humor, Stephanie Plum has many nasty encounters with the gritty, unsavory elements of crime novels rather than of comedies. And her quest for work is to keep herself, after her divorce, from sinking back into the family swamp like her supposedly "perfect" sister Valerie, who is anything but. It's clear that the Burg reveres women as domestic goddesses of the family dinner, home, and hearth. This is the fate Stephanie seeks to escape.

Who Wears the Baggy Pants?

But Lucille Ball's alter ego Lucy Ricardo and Stephanie have more in common than a camouflaged hunger for independence as well as commitment, and wild popularity. They have man problems.

Both Lucy and Stephanie *compete* with the men in their romantic lives. This is a feminist statement writ soft and subtle. The humor in both formats makes the women's unquenchable ambition for power far less threatening. Lucy competes for the public attention her performer husband gets. Amateur bounty hunter Stephanie Plum angles for the well-paying cases that cross into cop detective Joe Morelli's professional territory, and that's where both sexy interaction and infuriating differences show up. Only Stephanie, being single and a thoroughly modern heroine, has *two* men in her work and love life, not just one.

Altar Egos?

Here's Joe Morelli as seen early in *Two for the Dough*: "As a teenager Morelli had been feral. Two years in the navy and twelve more in the police force had taught him control, but I was convinced nothing short of removing his gonads would ever completely domesticate him. There was always a barbarous part of Morelli that hummed beneath the surface. I found myself helplessly sucked in by it, and at the same time it scared the hell out of me" (58).

Still, it's Joe's domestic possibilities—he maintains his own house, he loves her mother's home cooking, he claims to be true to her, maybe, plus he screws like a maniac—that keep Stephanie coming back. With Joe, it's sex. And love. Without the guaranteed commitment of marriage.

But Stephanie has a powerful ally, the mysterious good bad guy, Ranger. He is literally a Man in Black. Or camouflage colors on occasion. He's her go-to guy in a crunch, and the price is sex without love. But hot, great sex, and very tempting. And Ranger can be quite protective.

Here's where Stephanie's Lucy link is most obvious: Ranger is "the Cuban-American chameleon," as he's described on page one of *Two for the Dough*. It's that salsa-hot Latin lover thing again, and Italian-American stud Joe Morelli is just another flavor of the same fiery midsummer Jersey month.

Both men echo Desi's role: the handsome, dark, and volatile love interest on whose career-ground the heroine is always trespassing as heavy-footedly as a rogue elephant. Lucy has made her twin bed with Ricky Ricardo and will lie in it. But that was the fifties. Stephanie has made her bed mostly with neighborhood stud, detective Joe Morelli, but she may do or be in danger of doing an occasional overnight with Ranger, like any open-minded nineties girl enduring into the twenty-first century.

What is it with these hot Latin men, whether Italian-American or Cuban? And I don't mean billionaire basketball nerd Mark Cuban. I mean Cuban as it was in the 1940s before Castro and the fifties took over that island nation. Hot music, hot men, hot moves. That's what forties movies showed, along with all those exotic Latin dances like the tango and samba. The rage for Latin lovers made the career of *Ricardo* Montalban for sixty years. The rage for Latin rhythms made it likely for a Hollywood babe like Lucille Ball to marry Cuban bandleader Desi Arnaz, who played an onscreen Cuban bandleader named Ricky *Ricardo* in *I Love Lucy*. Is it any wonder that Stephanie Plum's mentor, protector, and sometimes seducer, Ranger, has a seldom-used real name that is *Ricardo* Carlos Mañoso?

The Split-Hero Syndrome

While Joe Morelli more thoroughly fits into the Ricky Ricardo mold, Ranger can never be counted out. Terse, hunky, sexy, and mysterious where Joe is high-handed, volatile, and openly after Stephanie (and has been since she was six), Ranger embodies the dark side of the Alpha male that Stephanie and many women can't resist, or ever quite trust. Morelli's no slouch as far as that dark side goes either—although, unlike Ranger, he's on the right side of the law.

The most universally recognized split-hero instance of our time is the fair-haired boy Luke Skywalker and the devil-may-care Han Solo of the Star Wars films. Idealistic Luke (Lucas from creator George Lucas's subconscious) must grow and ultimately face his Dark Side inheritance, but swashbuckling realist Han Solo gets the girl. Contemporary detective fiction exploits this divide constantly: Robert Parker's Spencer and his chillingly dangerous ally, Hawke, have spawned several good-guy shamuses with psychopathic pals to do the really dirty wet work.

Janet has gifted Stephanie with two Alpha males, but Joe Morelli clearly has more domestic promise. This lifelong womanizer with "a tongue like a lizard" (*One for the Money* 3) often states he's been off the woman hunt, despite Stephanie's suspicions to the contrary. He owns his own house and takes care of it. Ranger has "cribs," hidden and multiple. Morelli and marriage may be a possibility. Ranger and carnage and carnality are a certainty.

Yet both Lucy's and Stephanie's men have a strong ethnicity in common. Morelli is that volatile Italian with a capital East Coast *I*. Ranger is that cool Cuban with the hot hands. Both are close cousins to hot-tempered Cuban Ricky Ricardo.

Yet Stephanie is ninety degrees away from Lucy on the domestic front. Although she springs from domestically inclined folks, she resists losing her independence to marriage. She loves to eat but she's not wild to cook. She goes cookie-eyed at babies, but she loves to wear her spandex.

Her first unforgotten neighborhood encounter with Joe Morelli was when she was six and he took her into the garage to play "choo-choo." She resented the incident. Even then, Stephanie Plum hankered to play the part of "train," rather than "tunnel." They've been fighting for the role of "engineer" ever since.

On both fronts, though, Lucy and Stephanie's interference in their men's workday lives can make the guys as hopping mad as Bugs Bunny makes Porky Pig. In both cases, we're back to a cartoon comedy world where Stephanie has some updated and very special stooges and sidekicks of her own.

Lula: Ethel Mertz, on Speed and Fully Armed

A sidekick is as necessary an accessory for a crime novel as it is for a slapstick comedy. What would Hardy be without Laurel? Robert Parker's Spencer without Hawke? Stephanie without her gal pal? Only Stephanie's Ethel has a Lucy-like name: Lula.

In *Three to Get Deadly*, Lula swaggers from minor character into Stephanie's full field of vision and never leaves. A black woman of size and a former "ho," Lula operates under a dark history: being nearly beaten to death by a pimp. Where Lucy's sidekick, landlady Ethel Mertz, was a famously frumpy housewife, Lula wears the outrageously gaudy clothing that Evanovich carefully keeps away from Stephanie, who dresses sporty or T-shirt casual unless her job requires her to gussy up as reasonably female. (Steph does clean up well and don't Morelli and Ranger know it.)

Lula is a spandex sausage ready literally to explode out of her gaudy garments, possibly with a drawn firearm. She remains permanently plump, like Ethel Mertz, and therefore no sexual competition.

Stephanie's Big Fat Sugar Plum Fairy

The seven-foot-tall hairy transvestite who goes by the name of Sally Sweet and becomes a running secondary character is not only a combination sidekick and comic relief figure, but an early big fat clue to *I Love Lucy*'s impact on the author.

In season one of *I Love Lucy*, in an episode called "The Diet," Lucy struggled to lose twenty pounds in four days to fit into the costume of an ailing performer in Ricky's band. Featuring such bits as Lucy competing with the family dog for a table scrap, the episode showed Lucy eventually "steaming" off the weight. She made the show, doing a double-song number with Ricky, "Cuban Pete" and "Sally Sweet."

The number was cheeky and sexy and comic. The lyrics said they call her Sally Sweet, "the Queen of Delancey Street." Both Lucy and Desi went "chick-chicky-boom, chick-chicky-boom" plenty in the number. At one point a bump from Lucy's hip knocked off Ricky's hat.

Lucy's attempts to reemerge in the glamour of show business often exploited the actress's great looks and figure. But then something would go wrong and the beautiful face turned into the rubber distorted visage of a slapstick comedy clown; the inventive and energetic woman broke down in loud, ugly, childlike bawling. Professional ambition evolved into pratfall.

Stephanie the bounty hunter doesn't bawl, but she does show fear as well as tenacity, and she is beset by routine mayhem in the form of blown-up vehicles, often those snatched from Morelli or lent by Ranger. And all that slapstick keeps the men in her life, and everyone else in the Burg, from taking her or her bounty hunting seriously.

Guns and Neuroses and Fast Food

Stephanie brings a Lucy Ricardo innocence to using the tools of her bounty hunter trade. While Stephanie rarely carries and even more rarely successfully uses a firearm, she's surrounded by people who pull Glocks and other semi-automatics at the drop of a hamster. Interestingly, the armed and dangerous good guys in the Stephanie Plum books (besides Ranger and Morelli) are the minorities and disenfranchised: African-American Lula, the "almost dead" old folks in Stephanie's apartment building and her irrepressible Grandma Mazur, menopausal women, gay guys. None of these characters except the beloved Grandma Mazur would have been able to openly play a role on *I Love Lucy*.

Stephanie keeps her gun in a cookie jar, an old PI trick going back even farther than James Garner in *The Rockford Files*, but here the reference also relates back to family, and food that's bad for you. Her mother's tasty comfort-food family dinners and desserts are tools of emotional control, drawing Stephanie (and even Morelli on occasion) home to her mildly (and sometimes wildly) dysfunctional family: barely there father...man-, gun-, and corpse-obsessed Grandma Mazer...put-upon housewife mother hoping for the same for her daughter, a decent job and a decent man...and, later in the series, flaky divorced sister Valerie and her flakier love life. The family home front is also a place of confinement and living up to other people's expectations, just as the apartment of bored and desperate housewife Lucy Ricardo was.

And Stephanie's big, bad boy tool of professional control is often left home alone in the kitchen sweets jar.

Lucy's Daughters

Janet Evanovich's Stephanie Plum is still an infant, culture-wise, but she's had a mighty impact on contemporary mysteries with sassy female protagonists and has established a publishing franchise that usually only accrues to major male bestselling authors.

Like Fran Drescher's comic turn in *The Nanny* television series, Stephanie's bounty hunter has guts, a big heart and big hair, sexy Jersey Girl aplomb, and lives large.

Which means that they both have a lot in common with that desperate housewife of a much earlier era, the beloved and iconic Lucy Ricardo. (In fact, Viewers for Quality Television called *The Nanny* the nineties' version of *I Love Lucy*. *The Nanny* debuted in the fall of 1993 and the first Stephanie Plum novel, *One for the Money*, came out in 1994, so they were coinciding phenomena. But Drescher's *Nanny* character is TV history now, while Stephanie Plum is still conquering bestseller lists.)

Unlike the domestically anchored *Nanny* character, Stephanie Plum headed for the mean streets of the Burg from the get-go, installing herself firmly in the crime/mystery camp. It's not until *To the Nines*, though, that Stephanie herself notes that her bounty hunter retrievals have more to do with Lucy Ricardo than with her childhood icon Wonder Woman.

As the series continues, so will the high and low comedy. All Stephanie ever needs is a few bounty hunter dollars more to keep body and soul and hamster Rex together...and to decide whether she will domesticate enough to marry hunky but "feral" cop Joe Morelli, or to boff mysterious mentor with macho muscle, Ranger.

Hey, that's not a bad life plan for any woman, Stephanie. As Ranger would say, "It's sure worked for you, babe."

Award-winning ex-journalist and novelist **CAROLE NELSON DOUGLAS** is the literary chameleon behind fifty novels in several genres. Her Irene Adler Sherlockian novels of historical suspense were the first to introduce a woman from the Doyle Canon as a protagonist and won a *New York Times* Notable Book of the Year citation. Her Delilah Street, Paranormal Investigator, urban fantasy-mystery *Dancing with Werewolves* debuts in November.

The nineteen-book Midnight Louie series (*Cat in a Red Hot Rage*, etc.) features four human crime solvers abetted by a feline detective who writes his own chapters. Janet Evanovich described this Sam Spade with hairballs as "the funniest, hairiest, hard-boiled PI on the planet!" Ain't no Vaseline on him, either.

LAUGHING HER WAY
OUT OF TROUBLE

Kyra Davis

Just got laid off? Just found your husband cheating on you with his secretary? At least you don't have Stephanie's life. It's hard to take your own problems seriously while Stephanie's oil-wrestling naked FTAs and getting cars blown up left and right. Stephanie can't even take her own problems seriously. And that quality, Kyra Davis says, is the most important part of Stephanie's charm.

As a GENERAL RULE, rapists aren't funny.

The same could be said of domestic violence, kidnapping, custody suits, torture, and murder... unless, of course, you're talking about a Stephanie Plum novel. If that's the case, then those things frequently become hysterical. It's not that Janet Evanovich tries to make the act of rape itself funny, but her gift (and the gift she gives Stephanie) is that she can horrify you with the details of a violent crime in one paragraph (a newly discovered dismembered body, a vivid description of a particularly horrific assault) and have you rolling in the aisles in the next.

Yeah, I know, all this going back and forth between danger and humor doesn't in and of itself make Stephanie unique. Heroes and heroines have been playing that tune since Errol Flynn started cracking jokes while wearing Robin Hood tights. Any one who has read J. R. R. Tolkien knows that his characters are always good for a laugh in between their frequent near-death experiences. And of course, thirty- and forty-somethings will recall that Magnum PI solved crime while wearing loud Hawaiian shirts and a wry smile (at least I think it was wry, it was hard to see under the eighties-style furry mustache). But the difference is that Magnum PI compartmentalized his life. There were times when he was out there chasing down bad guys, saving damsels in distress, and getting out of life or death situations in the nick of time. Then there were times when he was hanging out with his friends, cruisin' in his borrowed Ferrari, and giving Higgins a hard time. When immersed in the latter, Magnum was charming, cute, and often quite funny. But he was pretty darned serious when he and his current love interest (and I'm using the L-word loosely) were running for their lives.

On the other hand, the first time we see Stephanie running for *her* life, she and Joe Morelli, her current *lust* interest (lust being the only L-word Stephanie used in association with Morelli until at least book five), are being chased by a possibly murderous prize fighter. As the scene unfolds we get a peek into Stephanie's mind. What is she thinking about?

She's thinking that Kathleen Turner is significantly more adept at looking sexy while hauling ass in a mini skirt and heels than she is. It's enough to make any reader giggle. A few sentences later, Stephanie makes a half-hearted attempt to arrest Morelli, and the manner and timing of this are so ridiculous and unexpected that the giggle turns into a laugh.

Stephanie even has us laughing three paragraphs after we see her narrowly avoid being raped in front of a room full of men by a 250-pound psychotic. That's an impressive feat.

How does Evanovich do it? Perhaps she has a worldview that lends itself to this kind of bizarrely entertaining fiction. Maybe she's prone to severe mood swings and she's using her protagonist's amusingly chaotic life as a literary manifestation of her own emotional instability. Or *maybe* she's grounded enough in reality to know this is how life really is. It's awful, it's hilarious, it's disgusting, and it's delightful, all at the same time.

Every so often we find ourselves laughing at something that would normally be considered an unfortunate event. If you've ever chuckled while reading one of the Darwin Awards, you're guilty of this—even if you suppressed your giggles and vowed to repent for your moment of inappropriate mirth by dedicating the next week of your life to prayer and community service. When reading a Stephanie Plum novel you can laugh without guilt. There's no way around it; her endless series of problems are just flat out funny.

Many of Evanovich's readers immediately recognized her genius and were inspired to invent their own self-deprecating heroines (myself included). And shows such as *Desperate Housewives* have proven that television heroines are also quite capable of making *us* laugh while *they* face danger. But Stephanie is the gal that got that particular ball rolling. And as balls go, it's a good one. Despite the media's insistence on categorizing this kind of entertainment as fluff, books like Evanovich's teach us something important. Humor is what makes the bad times bearable. We don't need to feel guilty about that. Rather, we should embrace it the way Stephanie does.

Case in point: A few years ago I went to my synagogue to hear a Holocaust survivor speak about his life. He was well into his eighties, and he had a wonderful disposition and a sparkling sense of humor. More than once he was able to elicit the audience's laughter. Eventually a woman raised her hand and asked the obvious question: How can you go through that kind of hell and emerge with your humor intact?

He looked her in the eye and said with a somber smile, "Think of the alternative."

That man had a choice. He could have chosen to spend his life in a fog of depression; God knows his melancholy would have been justified. But his strength of character allowed him to escape the despair that otherwise would have consumed him, like it would have done to so many of us had we been in his situation. Instead this man decided to enjoy the time he had left on this earth.

Of course, Stephanie's a little different. She hasn't seen the kind of evil the man at the synagogue bore witness to and she obviously isn't going to touch our souls in the same way. But she does speak to us, and she does make a lasting impression as she bungles her way through crime-fighting wearing platform shoes and cotton spandex tops. Will any of us forget the scene in which she forces her way into the home of a man who is wanted for beating his wife only to end up rolling around on top of his pizza while trying (unsuccessfully) to apprehend him? The poor girl is forced to spend the rest of the day picking pepperoni out of her hair. Spousal abuse is a serious issue and the man she was trying to capture was a revolting excuse for a human being, but it's hard not to smile when he escapes while wearing her handcuffs not once, not twice, but three times. And it's impossible not to empathize with Stephanie when she finds herself more concerned with the welfare of her cuffs than of the man wearing them.

But perhaps you're not convinced that this kind of humor is applicable to real life situations. Sure, the man who survived the concentration camps is able to crack jokes *now*: what was his disposition like in the thirties and forties?

For the record, I find it hard to believe that there was a lot of laughing going on at Dachau. But I do know it's possible to laugh while your life is falling apart. That's something I learned firsthand.

Five years ago I was a newly single mom struggling to find a way to support myself and my two-year-old son. My ex-husband is bipolar and in the years preceding our divorce he managed to go on enough manic spending sprees to leave me with tens of thousands of dollars of credit card debt. I was unaware of most of his lavish purchases because the things he was spending his money on (stocks on margin, futures in Montdavi Reserve, and so on) were intangible and he was having the bills sent to a P. O. Box. However, we lived in a community-property state, so the debt was as much mine as it was his. It didn't matter whether I knew about it beforehand or not.

When I originally got married I had an image of what my future was going to be like. I would spend my life married to the man that I loved who, as luck would have it, seemed to be on the verge of becoming very successful. He was caring and funny and after a few years together we created a beautiful son whom I originally assumed we would raise together in our picture-perfect life. Instead, my now-ex-husband committed a multitude of white-collar felonious crimes, was arrested twice for drunk driving, and after sticking a metal shish kabob sheer through his hand, got himself temporarily institutionalized. This life was something less than picture-perfect.

So when Nicole, a friend whom I had lost contact with during the early days of my marriage, shot me an e-mail in an attempt to reconnect, she was understandably a little out of the loop.

"Kyra," her e-mail began, "I haven't seen you since the wedding! I gave you that blender so you and your hubby could take me out on that sailboat of yours and make me margaritas on the bay! When's that going to happen, huh?"

I hesitated for a moment before responding, "Hmm, a margarita-making-blender on a sailboat with my hubby. Sounds fabulous. But I have one itsy bitsy problem: of all the things you just listed, the only thing I have left is the blender."

To this day Nicole repeats this tale to everyone who needs cheering up and it inevitably makes them laugh. It made me laugh, too, and thank God for that because laughing was one of the main things that got me through that time.

I had a lot of "Stephanie moments" during what I now think of as the "reconstructionist years" of my life. There were times when I feared my ex would try to get into my house while I was out so I would post signs on the door stating that I was fumigating and that anyone who entered risked being poisoned right along with the fleas and the spiders. And then there was the time when my ex called to tell me that he had a gun and that he wasn't safe with it. He then claimed that he was coming over so that I could take it away from him. I hung up the phone feeling fairly certain that this was his way of trying to guilt me into dropping the divorce and taking care of him. Still, being fairly certain is not the same as being beyond-a-shadow-of-a-doubt positive, so I decided that this was a good time to grab the kid and head to a nearby Starbucks. But before I got out the door the phone rang. It was my "transition man," whom I had gone out with the night before. It was clear from the suggestive tone of his voice that he wanted to use the call to relive our most recent make-out session. Obviously I wasn't in the mood for phone sex so I swallowed my irritation and said sweetly, "I'm really glad you had a good time last night, but I'm expecting my husband in a few minutes and apparently he's packing a loaded gun so would it be okay if I called you back?"

So you see, I am intimately familiar with Stephanie's brand of crazy. But Stephanie's better than me. *Stephanie* never lets me down. Because there were plenty of days when I didn't see the humor in my own misfortune. Days when the Paxil just wasn't cutting it. But Stephanie is never in anything but top form. When she discovers that a man has been sawed in half and deposited in her living room she still has the presence of mind (if you can call it that) to make a sarcastic remark about the death cooties that have now infested her sofa. When an interview subject shows her evidence of the middle finger that was "accidentally" severed earlier in the day, Stephanie pushes aside the urge to faint and remarks that the middle finger is her favorite finger of all. This woman has me laughing about a severed finger!

And that's the other thing that Stephanie gives us. When our lives are too dark for her to inspire us to laugh at our own problems, she gives us the opportunity to feel better by laughing at hers.

Personally, I found that when things were bad for me I didn't really want to read Elie Wiesel and Fredrick Douglass. I didn't need to read a book to get depressed; all I had to do to achieve *that* was read my Visa bill. It was my mother who recommended *One for the Money*. By that time Evanovich had already hit the number one spot on the *New York Times* bestseller list several times over, yet I had been too busy re-reading the classics to notice. I remember the first night I pulled back the front cover. It was past two in the morning and I was way too anxious to sleep. I needed a distraction and I remember eyeing the book suspiciously and grumbling that it better not be one of those "romantic suspense" novels. The last thing I needed was to read about some chick being rescued by her knight in shining armor and then riding off into the sunset while straddling the back of his white steed. I'd rather read about the slave trade.

On the first page of *One for the Money* we learn that Joe Morelli took Stephanie's virginity and then walked out of her life without a second thought. It was clear from the way Evanovich was setting it up that Stephanie and Joe's relationship wasn't over and I gritted my teeth as I waited for their romance to re-blossom.

And then on page four Stephanie Plum intentionally ran Morelli over with her car. She just drove up on the sidewalk and rammed right into him. And when he howled that his leg was broken, she smiled and drove off.

This, I thought, is my kind of woman.

Stephanie Plum isn't a hardboiled detective. If she were, her first adventure wouldn't have grabbed me the way that it did. What I needed then was a protagonist who was quirky, able to laugh at herself, and vain enough to care about her appearance—a woman like me. And I wanted that woman to kick some serious butt. I wanted her to knock Mr. Wonderful off his horse and put him in his place, and I wanted her to stand up to all her demons and destroy them, and I wanted to cheer her on while she did it. And in addition to all that, I wanted to laugh. That's really what it comes down to: when things were at their worst, Stephanie made me laugh. Stephanie isn't a mother of a two-year-old, nor does she have to contend with a men-

tally unstable ex with a gun. Yet there's always at least one person trying to kill her, and through all her near-misses she continues to make
us smile. That's what I call a life lesson.

Stephanie's not going to change our world views. She's not going
to bring tears to our eyes by pointing out the tragic and unjust suf-
fering of the underprivileged. There are lots of other literary protagonists that can do that for you and I strongly suggest you seek them
out. But then, once you're suitably outraged and depressed, pick up
a Stephanie Plum novel. She's not an intellectual. She's just fun—and
fun is something we can *all* use a little more of.

KYRA DAVIS is the author of the critically acclaimed novels, *Sex,
Murder, And A Double Latte, Passion, Betrayal, And Killer Highlights*,
and *So Much for My Happy Ending*. She has spent her life in San
Francisco and the Greater Bay Area where she currently lives with
her young son. During her free time she indulges in lattes, frappuc-
cinos, and anything else that will feed her caffeine addiction. Learn
more about her by visiting her Web site at www.kyradavis.com.

THE BAD BOY NEXT DOOR

AN OPEN LETTER TO STEPHANIE PLUM

Shanna Swendson

Stephanie, Shanna Swendson would like to have a word with you—about Joe Morelli. You know, Morelli? The guy who brings you pizza and tells you he loves you? The guy who knows your family almost as well as you do, and still wants to marry you? The guy who was your first—and who Shanna thinks also ought to be your last.

DEAR STEPHANIE,

I know you don't know me, but I'm a big fan. I've been following your adventures (and misadventures) for some time now, so I feel like I know *you* pretty well. I hope you don't think I'm being presumptuous in offering you a little advice, girlfriend to girlfriend.

I have just one thing I really want to say to you, and it's important: Wake up and smell the doughnuts and coffee! You may have managed to snag the perfect man, and unless you realize that and quit dithering, you may lose him.

Seriously, Steph (mind if I call you Steph?), what more could you want in a man than what you have in Joe Morelli? He's basically a combination of every female fantasy—a bit bad boy, a bit boy next door, a bit tough guy, a bit best buddy. Not to mention the fact that he's hot for your bod, no matter how many doughnuts you eat.

Okay, so maybe I'm not the best person to be offering anyone relationship advice. I haven't exactly had a lot of luck in that area (but then, I've never met a Joe Morelli). However, I know a thing or two about romance and relationships. I write about them all the time. Yeah, what I know may be stuff that only works in fiction, but considering the fact that you and Joe happen to be fictional, I think you could consider me an expert on the subject.

We writers have ways of classifying heroes. Different kinds of men fulfill different kinds of fantasies and star in different kinds of stories. There are your Alpha Males, the domineering, take-charge leaders who forge ahead to meet their goals and expect the world to jump when they say jump. On the surface, that doesn't sound like Mr. Fun, but these guys tend to be very successful. They're good at what they do, and money often comes with that. They're also just as focused on their relationships as they are on their other goals. If this kind of man wants you, you'll know it. He'll do just about everything in his power to win you over, and once he has you, he'll protect you as though you're part of his pack.

Then there are Beta Males. These are the best buddies of the world. They're loyal and dependable, even if they aren't quite as driven or successful as the Alpha Males. They're caring and sensitive, and there's never a doubt that they'll be there for you when you need them. The Beta Male is a guy you can call in the middle of the night when you have car trouble (like, perhaps, your car blowing up) or think you've heard a noise in your apartment, and he'll be right there. He's someone you can talk to who might actually listen, the guy you can watch the game with over pizza and beers.

Meanwhile, there's the common fantasy of the Bad Boy, the guy who needs taming—and who might be tamed by the right woman. He's got some rough edges, but he's a survivor. You can count on him to get himself out of any situation, no matter how rough, and to get you out of it, as well. He's exciting and maybe a little bit dangerous, but never, ever boring. He's hot and sexy and good for plenty of sleepless nights (in more ways than one, if you know what I mean).

But we also dream of the Boy Next Door, the one with a background similar to ours who blends in with our family and friends. You can invite him to your sister's wedding without worrying about him hooking up with one of the other bridesmaids, and your only fear about inviting him home for dinner is that your family will embarrass you in front of him. He's warm and comforting, and there's something about him that makes you feel safe and secure.

So, Steph, do any of these sound familiar? How about all of them? Let's take a look at Joe.

He's got a lot of those Alpha Male traits. He may not be at the upper echelon in the Trenton police department, but give him time.

He already has the respect of his colleagues, who are willing to bend rules to accommodate him. Why else do you think the rest of the police force is so eager to keep an eye out for your well-being (well, other than the sheer amusement factor)? When Joe says to look out for Stephanie Plum, they do it. Even Ranger, an Alpha Male in his own right, will occasionally subject himself to Joe's leadership when your safety is in question. Joe just oozes command and authority. He's someone you know knows what he's doing.

I know that's probably one of your biggest issues with him. He expects you to obey him the same way his police colleagues do, and you don't like obeying anyone. Heck, you'll put yourself in direct danger just because you don't want to obey an order that's in your own best interest. Even if you want to lie low while crazed hired assassins are out to get you, the moment Joe tells you to lie low, you become possessed with an irresistible urge to head straight to the mall. But honestly, has Joe ever ordered you to do something that went against your safety and well-being? It might be worth considering this as a potential point of compromise, given that his sense of your preservation is a lot better than your own.

I'm not even sure he minds all that much when you argue with him and push back, except when it requires him to come to your rescue or puts him in a situation that inspires teasing from his colleagues. He might like it when people follow his orders, but he respects people a lot more when they have the guts to stand up to him. He admires your spirit and spunk, and the day you back down and do exactly what he says (they're forecasting sleet in hell that day) he'll probably be deeply disappointed.

But Joe isn't always giving you orders and bossing you around. He's got a lot of Beta Male qualities mixed in with those Alpha tendencies. If you're honest with yourself, you'll admit that he's probably your best friend these days. You and Mary Lou will always have a certain bond, but whom do you really turn to for companionship most of the time? Who's your hockey-watching buddy? Whom do you meet for pizza? And who gets to hear about your worries, concerns, and family crises? About the only things you don't talk to Joe about are Joe himself and Ranger—and your dilemma of having to choose between them.

When you have a crisis at an odd hour, who's almost always there to help—sometimes before you even call him? When you need a place to stay after the latest intrusion at your apartment, who takes you in? For crying out loud, the man adopted a huge dog with an eating disorder when nobody else wanted it—a dog you would have otherwise been stuck with. How much nicer could he get? When he's not bossing you around, he's awfully sweet to you. The way he kisses you on the top of the head and calls you "cupcake" certainly makes me sigh.

Yet Joe is certainly no wimp. He's got enough Bad Boy in him to prevent him from getting too soft. He comes from a rough bunch, and while he does seem to have broken the Morelli mold of men who drink to excess, cheat on their wives, and indulge in lives of crime, he hasn't left his roots behind entirely. There's enough danger in Joe to keep him exciting. He's got the enticing external qualities of the bad boy wrapped around the upstanding citizen, a generous helping of strong leader Alpha traits mixed in with the loyal, dependable Beta ones. In other words, he always looks like he needs a haircut, frequently needs a shave, and does really nice things for a T-shirt and a pair of jeans.

Then there's the sex thing. Let's face it; a lot of your issues with Joe have to do with your past, going all the way back to childhood and that infamous game of "choo-choo." There's also that time behind the case at the Tasty Pastry (followed by the Buick incident). So, okay, those weren't exactly prime examples of positive male behavior. He was kind of a jerk then. But he seems to have outgrown the worst of that without losing the good aspects.

In other words, he's still a bit of a sex maniac, but he seems to be limiting his sex mania to you, and, these days, you can never accuse him of not calling. You might even think of his rather colorful past as training, practice from which you now benefit. Although you don't always go into that much detail about your sex life with Joe, I certainly get the impression that you don't have much to complain about in that area. Except an occasional need for a little more sleep.

As a teenager, you ran over him with your father's Buick when he slept with you and then didn't call. Now, you seem to be almost as angry that he not only wants to see you again, but would also like to make it a permanent arrangement. Honey, when a man like that starts using the "M" word, you don't take it lightly. His type has a bad habit of running from commitment, and now he's willing to make one. You might have paranoid moments when you suspect he might be seeing someone else (totally understandable, given how your marriage with Dickie Orr ended), but have you ever actually caught him cheating on you? You may not be the greatest detective ever, but you do have a way of solving crimes. I'd think you'd be equally good at ferreting out infidelity. It doesn't even seem like he's trying to get much action during the "off" phases of your relationship. Meanwhile, it's not like you have a perfectly clean record in that area. (*cough* Ranger *cough*) Just sayin'.

In spite of all of Joe's tough-cop, motorcycle-riding ways, he's still in a lot of respects the Boy Next Door. He's from the same neighborhood, so he knows and understands your background and you know and understand his. Because of this, you don't have to put on airs with each other; you're free truly to be yourself with him. You've known each other since you were kids (perhaps a little too intimately for that age, thanks to that game of choo-choo). You know his family, which I'll admit may or may not be a great thing, but on the other hand, he also knows your family and hasn't run away screaming yet. Now that your mother knows he isn't like the other Morelli men, he's a welcome guest at your family dinners, and he seems not only to tolerate but actually enjoy the zaniness of the Plum clan. His Grandma Bella may be kind of scary, and she and Joe's mother may not be crazy about the two of you living in sin, but they seem to have accepted you. At least they bring over casseroles, which in the Burg probably counts as a peace offering.

Joe owns his own house, and in the general area where you both grew up, so he's got a degree of respectability and stability. He's a military veteran. He's known in the community. He has a steady job with room for advancement. I bet he even votes. You two certainly seem to have more of the practical aspects of a relationship going for you than your sister and her latest man—and they even have a baby together.

And that seems to be the sticking point: babies and the potential thereof. If Joe were just an Alpha Male Bad Boy (more like Ranger, in other words), this might not be such a big issue for you. He wouldn't be so interested in settling down and starting a family, which means he also wouldn't be so set on you not being a bounty hunter. There aren't a lot of men who'd want the mother of their children to spend her days chasing and being chased by bad guys. A dad wants cookies in the cookie jar, not a gun, whether it has bullets in it or not.

Life sure would be easier for you if Joe didn't have those Beta Male and Boy Next Door qualities. He might still boss you around, but you'd get the hot sex and the excitement without being pressured for commitment. He'd be glad that you weren't exactly eager to quit being a bounty hunter, settle down, and have babies. He'd be a lot more like, well, Ranger. And how's that working out for you?

Apparently, the sex there was really good (although you told us a lot less about it than you tell us about your nights with Joe—might that be significant?). He's also good at showing up when he's needed and taking care of your messier work-related problems. He keeps you protected, even when it sometimes seems like it's his team that needs protection from you. He's even given you refuge, and work when you needed the money.

But there's also a lot he isn't giving you. He's told you he doesn't want a commitment, that he doesn't want a big-R relationship. He's not really someone you can talk to or hang out with. He has a past you've only seen glimpses of, and his present is almost equally hidden from you. You don't even know where he lives. Ranger's not the least bit interested in becoming more involved with your family than he already is. It seems to me that if you really wanted the kind of relationship you think you want with Joe—sex, companionship, no demands, no commitment, no babies—you could have it with Ranger, and you'd have jumped on that by now instead of playing coy and sidestepping the issue whenever Ranger gives you the slightest touch.

So, what is it that you're scared of? You've got the perfect Alpha/Beta Bad Boy Next Door who thinks you're incredibly sexy and wants to marry you, and the closer he gets, the more you want to run away. Is it the thought of the wedding itself, which, let's face it, carries with it the potential for supreme disaster (given your track record with things like fires and explosions and your oddball collection of family and friends)? Is it the thought of having babies and all the responsibility that comes with them (a lot more than comes with a hamster)? Is it worries about Joe himself? Or is this all about your sense of independence?

If it's the latter, I can relate. I'm older than you are (though, oddly enough, I was younger than you when I started following your adventures) and I'm still unattached. When you've lived alone long enough, giving up that independence to merge your life with someone else's is scary. It's probably even scarier for you, considering what happened the last time you made a commitment to a man. Anyone who walks in on her husband with another woman so soon after the wedding has a right to be more than a bit altar-shy.

But the real point of contention between you and Joe seems to revolve around your career. While I normally wouldn't suggest that a woman choose a man over her career, you do have to consider both the man and the career, and in your case, one is a real prize while the other isn't so much. It might be time to think about a small compromise.

I've already listed Joe's good points. Now let's look at your job. You work for a weasel (or someone who'd be willing to have intimate relations with a weasel, which is basically the same thing). You spend your time tracking down criminals, which means going into unsavory places. You've been shot at, you've lost count of how many of your cars have been blown up (though I'm sure your insurance company is keeping a tally), and people walk in and out of your apartment at will, sometimes leaving dead bodies behind them. You've had contracts taken out on your life. You've been kidnapped.

And, let's face it: while you do usually manage to solve the big cases, you're not that great at the day-to-day work of your job. How many bail jumpers have outsmarted you repeatedly? How many have driven away in your own car, with your purse in it? How many times have you found yourself wrestling with naked drunks (and not in a good way)? How often do you find yourself smeared in food, dirt, trash, or worse? Doesn't sound like something you should risk losing a great man for to me.

I'm not saying you have to resort to the button factory or tampon plant. But maybe you could find something that gives you the same burst of excitement you get from bounty hunting with fewer of the unpleasant aspects of the job. You don't have to go all-or-nothing and be a housewife, like Joe has suggested. I'm sure if you talked to him about this, he'd be willing to compromise as well, and be open to you working as long as it's work that doesn't involve sirens, guns, and every police officer in Trenton knowing what you're up to. After all, he does have those Beta Male and Boy Next Door qualities. He may seem stubborn and domineering, but he is capable of talking things out.

So, Steph, the bottom line seems to be that you've got a man who embodies just about all of the qualities that we women look for—even the seemingly contradictory ones. He's come a long way from his upbringing to become a man worthy of you. Would it be so bad for you to make a few changes in your life to accommodate him?

Come to think of it, though, if you ever do change jobs and settle down with Joe Morelli, it would probably end your adventures and deprive me and millions of other people of hours of amusement. On second thought, never mind. Forget everything I've just said.

Your friend,

Shanna

SHANNA SWENDSON is the author of *Enchanted, Inc.* and *Once Upon Stilettos* and has contributed to the Smart Pop anthologies *Flirting with Pride and Prejudice*, *Welcome to Wisteria Lane*, and *So Say We All*. She has conversations with fictional people more often than is probably healthy, but usually they're with her own characters.

A LITTLE LESS CONVERSATION

A BABE'S VIEW

(OR WHY I'M A WHUMPA WHUMPA GIRL...
AND STEPHANIE IS, TOO)

Donna Kauffman

Talking's so overrated. Just ask Donna Kauffman—one literary look from Ranger, and her heart goes into overdrive. Stephanie is the same way. But that's not the only reason, Donna says, that Stephanie should choose Ranger over Morelli....

"BABE," HE SAYS.

Until *Twelve Sharp*, that pretty much summed up Ranger's entire vocabulary. That one word, uttered as only Ranger can utter it, and Stephanie immediately wants to get naked. In fact, he can have that effect with no language at all. Just a look will do. Hell, just standing there, breathing, really.

The thing is, I don't even know the guy, and *I* want to get naked. Not while Stephanie is naked with him, of course. I mean, I admire the hell out of her spunk, her determination, and her bravery, not to mention her willingness to risk the ultimate act of sacrifice every time she gets behind the wheel of a car, any car. But I don't want to get naked with her. I'm assuming the feeling would be mutual. After all, if Stephanie gets cold at night, she has Joe Morelli. And Bob the dog, for that matter. If I were her, I'd choose the dog over me. And not just because that leaves more naked Ranger for me. Okay, mostly because that's exactly what that means. But I'd go to greater lengths than pawning off a smelly dog to secure my naked future with that man.

Ah, that man. That elusive, shrouded-in-mystery-and-black-cammies Ranger. Just Ranger. One name. Okay, so we know his whole name now: Ricardo Carlos Mañoso. But no one is going call this guy

Little Ricky anytime soon. He'll always be just Ranger to us. That's all we need. And when I say we, I mean the hoards of women who would leave their husbands (boyfriends, significant others, country of origin, planet Earth...) tonight if they thought it would buy them five minutes of naked time with Ranger in his highly secure, seriously decadent penthouse suite. Or on the heated seats of his black Mercedes sedan. Or up against the nearest fence post.

What is it about this mostly monosyllabic male that makes our pulse pick up, our heart go pitty-pat...or whumpa whumpa, as the case may be? I'm a whumpa whumpa girl myself. In fact, Stephanie and I share that particular heart condition. Stephanie might be hard up for a car that remains in one piece, not to mention decent insurance rates, but she's not missing any men in her life. Ranger and Joe both want Stephanie. And, because she's not dead, blind, or stupid—although Joe might occasionally argue about the latter—Stephanie wants both of them right back.

The thing is, she's had them both. She's even lived with them both (the wench), at one point simultaneously, in her own apartment. And she's still torn.

In her defense, it would be a tough spot to find yourself in. Not that I would know personally, but a girl can dream. In my vivid and highly detailed imagination, I think about what it would be like to have, say, both Matthew McConaughey and Clive Owen pursuing me. Naturally, both would take me to bed and want to keep me there. And, being Alpha males, they wouldn't take kindly to me dragging out my decision by continuing my liaisons with both of them. Like Stephanie, I'd eventually be forced to make The Choice. What to do? Or, more to the point, who to do? It's a decision I know I'd struggle with. Okay, maybe "struggle" isn't the word. More like "ponder deliciously over a prolonged period of time and deep, up close and personal evaluation." But I could pretend to struggle. Especially if Clive was holding me down and taking his sweet time while doing the most incredible things to me with his—um, sorry, I digress.

Where was I? Oh yeah. Stephanie's Choice. Not tragic, like, say, Sophie's, but a major dilemma in the World of Plum. Stephanie isn't the only one struggling with this problem. We readers struggle with her choice, too. (Like we have nothing better to worry about. Like we all wouldn't like to have that problem.) I mean, I could do without homicidal boxers stalking me, mysterious bookies taking up sudden residence in my apartment, or having ever to apprehend a naked man coated in butter. But having to make The Choice? That I could stand. And I'm far from alone. Stephanie's Choice has led to the birth of The Debate. A sometimes heated, often animated global discourse held on Internet bulletin boards and in myriad chatrooms, analyzed in blogs, via cell phones, through reams of text messages, and probably somewhere by smoke signals.

Joe vs. Ranger. Whom should Stephanie choose?

Clearly I've made my choice, but we're not talking about my future with Ranger. (More's the pity.) What we're all endlessly and quite deliciously debating is whom Stephanie should exclusively spend her days (and nights) with. Who is the better man?

It seems an easy call on the surface. Why shouldn't Stephanie choose Joe, the domesticated police detective? Well, the potentially domesticated police detective.

Let's examine the evidence. I think it's very telling that with Joe Morelli, Stephanie is, essentially, a pitty-pat girl. Joe is well known in the Burg for his clever fingers and ability to charm the pants off members of the opposite sex. Literally. He was playing "choo-choo" with Stephanie when she was six and he was eight. Then he went on to steal her virginity ten years later behind the pastry display of the local bakery. Yes, yes, she ran him over with her Uncle Sandor's Buick a few weeks later just to let him know she wasn't a total pushover, but I think that's part of her charm in his eyes. In all our eyes, maybe. Bottom line, it's another ten years later and Joe can still get Stephanie into bed, with only the occasional risk of life and limb.

The thing is, if the bed (floor, table, pastry counter) is more than five feet away, there is a 50/50 shot that any number of things will happen between "let's have sex" and the two of them hitting the sheets that will prevent It from ever happening. He could get called to a crime scene. More often, something related to one of Stephanie's FTAs either shows up, blows up, burns down, or otherwise ruins her chances of getting laid.

Ranger, on the other hand, says, "Babe." Bullets could be flying, homicidal midgets could be fixing her in their sights. Hell, Rome could be burning one block over...and it's still wall-to-wall whumpa.

It doesn't matter how far away from a bed (wall, table, pastry counter) they might be. Ranger doesn't even require that there be floor space. Naked abandon can and will occur.

And yet, we can't simply tag Ranger with the Alpha male title and use that as his main appeal to the admittedly weak-whumpaed Stephanie. We've already established that Joe isn't exactly Beta. Or even Omega. He's a cop. A detective, for God's sake. A true first-line-of-defense, I-got-your-back kinda guy (which comes in really handy if you're Stephanie). That means we can't separate and judge Ranger or Joe's suitability as a life mate for Stephanie based solely on testosterone levels. It's more the crux of Stephanie's dilemma in being attracted to both of these two men than the ultimate deciding factor between the two. She is drawn to that specific aspect in both of their natures. (And honestly, who wouldn't be?) Though the Alpha trait manifests itself differently in each man, both have the Alpha gene carved into their DNA, Alpha with a capital A. Both are protect-and-defenders by nature and by profession. Both would kill to save Stephanie or make the ultimate sacrifice if the situation called for it. But here's where the crucial difference lies: Joe is a bad boy gone good. The same guy who convinced Stephanie to play choo-choo in his garage as a highly sexed eight-year-old is now a law-abiding, law-upholding cop. Joe is a life-long, Burg-dwelling, old home-restoration, home, hearth, and Bob kinda guy, with the requisite unwieldy Italian family and evil-eye casting grandmother to go with it.

Ranger, on the other hand, is…not. He is a bad boy who is still bad. Make that b-a-a-a-a-a-a-d with a capital B.A.D. He doesn't have a single thing in common with Joe's list. In fact, it's hard to imagine that Ranger even had a childhood, much less has a family tucked away somewhere. Sure, we know he has a long distance and somewhat distanced relationship with his little daughter, Julie. And he has family in the Burg somewhere. But, essentially, twelve books worth of adventures later, he's still an enigma, both to Stephanie and to us. He is a penthouse dweller, denoting a serious bottom line; footloose to the point of being exceedingly single, with a background of an ambiguous and potentially tragic nature; highly trained in wide-ranging skill sets by factions completely unknown to us (but definitely not a mail-order school); with, oh yeah, a trail of dead bodies behind him. Of course, they all deserved it. But still.

So, yes, in the Alpha vs. Alpha contest, Ranger wins. If you like that kind of thing.

(waving hand wildly)

Steph likes that kind of thing. It's why she continues to end up between Ranger's high-thread-count sheets even though she knows Joe is the take-home-to-mama kind of guy. Which brings up another point. Stephanie has brought Joe home for dinner on multiple occasions. He doesn't seem out of place at the Plum dining room table. Not completely. After all, Joe is a Burg guy. A Sunday-family-pot-roast-and-pineapple-upside-down-cake kind of guy. The kind of guy who'd be equally comfortable cracking open a beer and parking himself in front of the game with Stephanie's dad, or stepping into the kitchen to help with the dishes and perhaps cop a feel of Stephanie's butt with soapy dishpan hands. On occasion, he also comes in handy when Grandma Mazur waves firearms around the dining room table. Joe's a family guy. A Plum family guy, anyway.

We've seen Ranger in the Plum home exactly once. All intense and heavily armed—concealed, of course—sitting across from Stephanie's grandmother at the dining room table. I picture it in a sort of rubber necking, peeking-through-the-fingers-of-my-hands-as-I-cover-my-face kind of way. Actually, the idea of Stephanie trying to blend Ranger into the Plum household kind of excites me. (Anything involving mental images of Ranger, in any capacity, in any location, excites me, but I digress yet again.) Depositing Ranger at a standard Burg dining room table is like dropping a rare exotic creature into soccer mom suburbia. Does he adapt? Not really. Did Grandma Mazur take one look at him and want to get naked? Of course she did. (Okay, I have now officially discovered one mental image involving Ranger that does not excite me.)

So…what is it about Ranger that makes Stephanie whumpa whumpa while also-Alpha Joe gets a pitty-pat? It can't just be Bad Boy vs. Reformed Boy Next Door, because Joe is still no angel. He goes after what he wants, and what he wants a great deal of the time is Stephanie (though I think he's just as confused about why he wants her as I am). He doesn't always play fair when he wants Stephanie naked. And here's why: Sure, he wants her naked because he has an abundantly healthy sex drive (see choo-choo train game, age eight) but I'd hazard to guess that his determination to keep her in bed is also driven by the notion that the more time she spends naked in his bed, the less time she spends out blowing up her car or burning down Stiva's Funeral Parlor.

Which brings up my next issue. If all Joe Morelli wanted was sex, I doubt he'd have to look very far to find a willing partner. So why Stephanie? Why does he care? Sure, he's a cop, sworn to protect and defend, but I don't think he takes his job so seriously that he keeps her close by just so the citizens of Trenton can sleep easier at night. Why put up with her crazy antics?

In the Ranger vs. Joe debate, how the two men react to Stephanie's rather... *uneven* job performance issues is another key to solving the mystery of why Ranger might be better for Stephanie long-term than Joe. Think about it: Joe spends most of his time being exasperated with Stephanie. For which I don't fault him. If my on-again-off-again girlfriend spent her days chasing buttered naked guys and getting her car blown up on a routine basis, I would tend to get a little cranky, too. And yet, he remains reliable and faithful, always willing to bail her out, even if he does so with a heavy sigh and a major eye roll. And if he gets her naked within a reasonable amount of time afterwards, he's happy. But why? Why put up with Stephanie's wacky life? Not just for the sex. We've established he wouldn't have to look far for that. (Hello, Joyce Barnhardt?)

The thing with Joe is, he's a guy. A real guy. The everyday, go to work, get paid, come home, want a home-cooked meal and a little lovin' guy. Real guys don't want drama. They don't look for conflict. Sure, Stephanie lives in a swirl of constant drama, but she's a known quantity to Joe. And I think rather than start all over again with someone new, he'll just stick with the drama he knows, and hope that the law of averages finally swings his way. After all, just how many times can someone try to kill her? That, or she'll eventually agree to give up her bounty hunting job and go to work in the button factory. (Poor, delusional man.) So he sticks around. Despite everything. Even when, on the surface, it makes no sense. And for Stephanie, the pull of Joe is that very stability, that dependability, that normalcy. And Lord knows she could use some of that. Even if she doesn't understand why he stays, she's willing to put up with the heavy sigh of acceptance when she screws up—again—because it's nice having someone who won't leave, no matter what.

But—and pay attention, because this is the "light bulb" moment right here—Joe doesn't really get Stephanie. He loves her, yes, but he loves her despite her foibles, her ridiculous job, and the almost constant scrapes she gets herself into.

Ranger, on the other hand, wants her for exactly who she really is. And that right there, my friends, is why he's in the game. And why, when all is said and done, he's her man.

Ranger doesn't want Stephanie to give up the life of a bounty hunter, or her kooky friends, or the constant threat of danger. He completely gets the pull of that life. So rather than try and make Stephanie into something she's not—and she's not cut out to be a Burg wife, no matter her job description—he works to make her better at what she's already doing. Does he worry about her? Constantly. But rather than keep her locked up and out of trouble, he arms her and teaches her how to protect herself. He shows up when things go south and lends a hand. He doesn't make her feel inadequate but instead assumes that with the proper training and firepower, she could actually be good at this bounty hunting thing. When Ranger looks at Stephanie, no matter how bad the situation has gotten—and Stephanie can find new levels of bad without even trying—he watches her with this kind of affectionate amusement. He's just proud she's out there trying. He bolsters her self-esteem, rather than trying to undermine it.

Put it this way: Ranger would never put Baby in a corner.

And let's face it, Stephanie doesn't get that level of understanding from Joe . . . or anyone. Certainly not her family. Well, Grandma a little, but only because it gives her an excuse to carry concealed. And when it comes to dependability, Ranger is there for her in ways Joe can't be. He doesn't bat an eye over the situations she finds herself in. He knows stuff happens, and sometimes that stuff is really bad. He's always there. He has a vested interest in keeping her safe because he cares, but he doesn't judge and he doesn't complain. On the surface, it doesn't look like they'd have anything in common. But Ranger is the one guy who gets the real Stephanie, the Stephanie who is a Burg misfit, the Stephanie who has a bit of Bond Girl in her, the Stephanie who maybe, just maybe, has bigger things to do than marry and add to the Burg baby population. The Stephanie who kind of likes living in Ranger's penthouse suite and who could get used to those high-thread-count sheets.

So, it doesn't matter that he's not your everyday, average guy, that he's not marriage material, or the kind of man you want to take home to mama. Though trust me, mama wouldn't mind. Think about it. Once she got past the intimidating size and the arsenal...yeah, she'd want to get naked with him, too. It's a girl thing. A bad boy thing. She might never admit it out loud, but the moment he leaves the house, she'd be wondering when he was coming by again.

But mostly, mama wouldn't mind because all she'd have to do was see that look of affectionate understanding, that look of honest appreciation in his eyes when he looks at her daughter, and suddenly it wouldn't matter that his background is murky, his day-to-day activities less than savory, or possibly not even legal, that his substantial income probably goes unreported. She'd worry, but she'd get over it. Because it's rare you find a man who looks at you like that because he completely gets you. And she knows it.

And so do I.

So, Joe? You're a good man, with your heart in the right place. And in a perfect world, you and Stephanie would settle down and raise Bob and some babies and live happily ever after. But Stephanie isn't just that girl you played choo-choo with. And Ranger knows it. He can offer her something nobody else in her world can. So he's not going anywhere. And if Stephanie's smart, and I know she is, she'll make sure he stays right where he is.

If not...he can always call me. I'm ready to kick this suburban soccer mom thing and find my inner Bond Girl. Ranger is just the man I want to help me do that.

Sorry, Joe.

Babe...call me.

U.S.A. Today bestselling author **DONNA KAUFFMAN** has seen her books reviewed in venues ranging from *Kirkus* to *Library Journal* to *Entertainment Weekly*. A past RITA finalist, National Readers Choice, Maggie, and PRISM award winner, she lives in Virginia with her teenage sons and a growing menagerie of animals. Donna loves to hear from her readers. You can contact her through her Web site at www.donnakauffman.com.

EENY, MEENY, MINEY, MO

CAN STEPHANIE HAVE HER CAKE AND EAT IT TOO?

Nancy Tesler

Even if you aren't Stephanie, it's a difficult thing to decide be-
tween two men like Joe and Ranger. But let's take a minute,
put away the question of whom we think Stephanie should
choose, and ask: Why does she have to choose at all?

WHEN I WAS THIRTEEN my brother, six years my senior, caught
my best friend and me in the finished basement of our Worcester,
Massachusetts, home fooling around (in those days that meant serial
kissing) with a couple of boys we'd met some months earlier at a local youth center. It was New Year's Eve and my parents thought we
were downstairs playing ping pong.

"You'll get a *reputation!*" my appalled brother berated me. "No one
will ever date you for any other reason!"

Mortified at the prospect of being labeled a slut for all eternity, I
stifled the cravings of my burgeoning sexuality and refused to kiss
another boy for the next three years, thereby earning for myself a different kind of reputation, that of the biggest "prude" Classical High
had ever graduated. Between sixteen and eighteen I did allow an occasional chaste meeting of the lips, but my persona was firmly established and the boys I went out with knew better than to try anything
else. It was the fifties, and "nice" girls, it was pounded into our heads,
didn't.

No one could accuse Stephanie Plum, the product of a far more
sexually liberated generation, of anything resembling prudishness,
right? After all, she loses her virginity at age sixteen to Joe Morelli,
and she's in and out of his bed (also Ranger's, though only the one
time) from the fourth book in the series on. Yet I contend that here
she is at thirty, a divorced Generation-Xer, stuck with a similar kind

of middle-class, old-fashioned morality: blue-collar "Burb" morality, where the indoctrination begins at age five and can never totally be shaken. Ridiculous, you say? Times have changed. The pill and the sixties' sexual revolution have freed women from these kinds of shackles. Just as a man can go from flower to flower to flower, today's woman can flit from bee to bee to bee without fear of being called loose. Or of going to hell. No longer is a girl with a healthy sex drive like Stephanie's forced to sublimate her natural impulses.

Then why the long dry spell between Stephanie's divorce and the Morelli-inspired orgasm in book four? Why does she move out of his house shortly afterward because "I don't think I'm cut out for irresponsible sex" (*Four to Score* 208)? What prompts this flight to safety? What could brash, smart-mouthed Stephanie Plum possibly be afraid of? Not hellfire and damnation, surely. Well, maybe a tad. Never discount the influence of nuns. But there's something else at play here. Is it "fear of getting dumped again? Fear of getting screwed over? Fear of defective condoms" (*Four to Score* 194)? Or how about the specter of being given "the eye" by Morelli's Grandma Bella, a prospect I find a lot scarier than my brother's slut prediction?

Consider her history. The young Stephanie, deviating from her longstanding pattern of unconventional behavior, does the conventional thing and marries Dickie Orr. Dickie isn't wild like Joe Morelli. He isn't drop-dead, movie-star handsome like Joe Morelli. He doesn't attract women the way honey attracts bears—like Joe Morelli. Dickie is safe. Dickie will never break Stephanie's heart and make her want to run him over with a Buick. And Dickie is undoubtedly a good catch in the eyes of her relatives and friends. He's everything her family (with the exception of Grandma Mazur, who knows a horse's "patoot" when she sees one) could have wished for. Her mother can stop "tippling," secure in the knowledge that Dickie will clip her high-spirited daughter's wings so that she'll no longer be tempted to do the adult equivalent of jumping off a roof to see if she can fly. After all, he's a lawyer; not overly bright but bright enough to have made it through law school, expected to make a comfortable living, and probably capable of siring a multitude of Plum-Orr babies to keep his young wife barefoot and pregnant for the foreseeable future. Who could have guessed that what he wasn't capable of was keeping his fly zipped?

I was twenty-two and still a virgin when I married my Dickie Orr. He was an ambitious doctor/resident, very bright and dead-broke, but he was persistent, I was ready, and he came with my mother's seal of approval. Who could have guessed that he too was incapable of keeping his fly zipped? Admittedly, our situations aren't completely analogous. My Dickie did sire three children and the marriage lasted a lot longer than Stephanie's, partially because I was a lot dumber than she was and it was years before my rose-colored glasses came off, and partly because my Dickie was smarter than her Dickie and never got caught screwing on the dining room table. I suspect the couch in his office got a marathon workout over the years, but he had a well-trained receptionist so I was spared the ignominy of catching him, as Stephanie does, *en flagrante delicto*.

Stephanie has known Morelli since the time he lured her into his father's garage to play "choo-choo" when she was six years old and he was eight. Over the next ten years we're led to believe that she faithfully heeded her mother's admonition to "stay away from those Morelli boys" (*One for the Money* 3), all of whom had the well-deserved reputation of being philanderers and drunks. It's apparently in the genes and the young Joe Morelli showed no signs of breaking the mold. Stephanie had been warned. She wasn't six anymore. No way would she allow herself to be compromised by this undisciplined rake, no matter how hot he was. She was, she believed, firmly in control of her biological urges. Until that fateful afternoon when he walked into her bakery shop.

I was a freshman in college and living in New York when I met my Morelli. Charlie was tall and strikingly good-looking in the way of the black Irish, dark wavy hair, Caribbean blue eyes, a smile that gave me tachycardia—forget what it did to other parts of my anatomy— and a touch that set me ablaze. He was a year older than I, already a campus sex-symbol, and I couldn't believe he was interested in me. The fact that he was a different religion and that my mother disapproved only added to his forbidden-fruit appeal. We were both theater junkies and were cast opposite each other in *A Midsummer Night's Dream*. Could anything be more romantic? The hormones were clamoring at the gate but the Beatles hadn't yet "done it in the road," the drug scene was still a ways off, and torrid smooching was as far as I dared go. Unlike Morelli, poor Charlie never even got to cop a feel.

In those days, however, walking hand in hand up Fifth Avenue at Christmastime, caught up in the magic of the joy-to-the-world season, pausing now and again for a stolen kiss in the shadow of Saks or Tiffany's, was as exciting as Stephanie's encounter behind the éclair counter in the bakery. Every so often it crosses my mind that the bed-hopping generations that followed mine are missing out.

Not that I'd recommend turning back the clock.

In the course of my marriage there were one or two members of the opposite sex, usually actors with whom I was working, who set off a disquieting jumble of thrills and chills, causing a quandary not unlike the one Stephanie faces by the time we get to *Eleven on Top*. What does a woman do when she finds herself wanting two men at the same time? In my case, absolutely nothing. My brother's words, not to mention my marriage vows, were burned into my brain. Nice girls didn't cheat.

Stephanie, on the other hand, is single and free to choose between two of the sexiest, most charismatic men in modern fiction, or to tell them both to take a hike. In my opinion and in the opinions, I'm certain, of most of Evanovich's readers, she'd have to be brain-dead and hormonally challenged to walk away. So okay, why does she have to choose? In today's anything-goes society, can't she have her cake and eat it too?

Not easily. My guess is weight-control may have to fall by the wayside as she makes jelly doughnuts a permanent staple of her diet—sugar and carbs replacing bee-to-bee flitting—because despite her often out-of-control libido, she's stuck with that Burb morality thing. Plus, Joe Morelli and Ricardo Carlos "Ranger" Mañoso are not going to tolerate her waffling for long. These guys aren't known for their willingness to share anything, and certainly not a woman. At present they've formed a strange and uneasy alliance in an effort to keep her fingers attached to her hands and her brains from being splattered all over her parking lot. But a showdown is coming.

Will she choose or will she bolt?

From childhood, Stephanie's love/hate relationship with Morelli has consumed her fantasy life. Throughout her adolescence and well into her adulthood, his sexual exploits were the subject of endless gossip and speculation between Stephanie and her best friend, Mary Lou. If Morelli, in his hell-raising days, thought about her at all it was no doubt as a sex object, desirable as hell, but a one-night stand—and after she ran him down with the Buick, a crazy-as-a-bedbug pain in the ass. And that sentiment only intensifies when, after a stint in the Navy, he becomes a cop and runs into her in her bounty hunter capacity. But then there's the chemistry, the attraction that won't go away. Even after they finally do the deed and Stephanie starts imagining her cookie jar in his kitchen, she and Morelli still aren't on the same wavelength. Yes, she's got that great bod he never tires of exploring, and a mouth that, when she keeps it shut, demands to be kissed. But she's "Calamity Jane in fucking spandex!" (*Four to Score* 145). Enthusiastic as he is about getting her in his bed whenever possible, he'd have to be a masochist to consider marrying a disaster magnet whose cars keep getting blown to kingdom come. Then somewhere down the line the relationship takes a turn and the balance shifts. Suddenly Morelli is getting serious and Stephanie can't get the words "I love you" out of her mouth. She feels it, she says. She just can't say it. Why? Isn't this the guy she's secretly always wanted? Aren't they made for each other? Doesn't she go liquid whenever his brown eyes turn "melt-in-your-mouth chocolate" (*One for the Money* 4)? Isn't his name the one she deliberately picks out of a bowl when lust overcomes her and she wants out of her little black dress? She certainly has no complaints about his performance in the sack, and he's developed into a responsible grown-up and a good cop without losing any of his animal magnetism, so what is her problem?

Ranger, of course. Stephanie may have peeked when she picked Morelli's name out of the bowl, but Ranger's name was in there, too. In fact, it was the only other one. Ranger appeals to the little girl in her who still wants to fly on a magic carpet, and carpet-flying isn't something you do with a committed partner. As desirable as he is, Morelli is becoming a threat to Stephanie's independence. Morelli wants her out of the law enforcement business before one of the psychos she's always chasing manages to cut her up into little pieces and feed her to the fish. Morelli uses the L-word. And worse still, on odd days, the M-word. Ranger, on the other hand, is clearly not marriage material. Ranger is "smoke" (*Hot Six* 22). Ranger is the wind. Ranger finds her bizarre crime-fighting adventures entertaining, if at times a little disconcerting. He uses the L-word too, but with qualifications. Stephanie's pretty sure he's killed people. Several, in fact. He has a *past*. And a *secret*. He also has a daughter, and no one knows for sure where his home, "the Bat Cave," is. Ranger is mysterious, forbidden fruit, and Stephanie can't help fantasizing. She's had a bite of the apple, but only enough to whet her appetite, and it's possible that Ranger may prove to be the snake that's going to get her kicked out of Eden—i.e., Morelli's bed. He has the ability to totally screw up her life, and everyone knows Murphy's Law could have been based on Stephanie's life. If it can go wrong, she'll see to it that it will. Or will she?

If Stephanie chooses Morelli, what does she do about those electric shocks (and I don't mean the zaps you get from a stun gun) that raise the hair on the back of her neck whenever Ranger lays a finger on her? Could she possibly make her peace with staying home and making babies? The making part she'd undoubtedly enjoy, but how about all those diapers? Still, her biological clock is ticking away and she's beginning to have maternal feelings about dogs. If she chooses Ranger there'll be no babies or even dogs, and she'll be on a scary but exhilarating rollercoaster ride that may end with her being pitched over the side. Which brings to mind the safety factor again. Despite her penchant for getting into wacky, extraordinarily unsafe situations, Stephanie, like most women, longs to be with a man who makes her feel safe. With which one of these two men does she feel safer now? Well, it depends. If she's hiding from a psychotic killer, Ranger's well-guarded local residence with its Bulgari-smelling sheets is clearly the place to be. But on a day-to-day basis, I think it's in Morelli's arms.

When I was a biofeedback practitioner—that's a stress-reduction therapist—an exercise I instructed my clients to work on was finding a "safe haven," somewhere they could retreat to mentally when the stress in their lives got out of control. It could be a sandy beach or a remote cabin in the mountains or a childhood sanctuary such as a tree house. For me, in my "in love" days, that place was in my bed wrapped in my husband's arms. (The moral of that story, of course, is pay attention to red flags, don't fall in love with a wolf in sheep's clothing, and realize that the world isn't a very safe place and the only person who can make you feel even relatively safe is probably you.)

Maybe the only way for Stephanie to deal with her ambivalent feelings is to compromise—Ranger for the short-term, Morelli for the long haul. But that carries with it its own set of problems. Can Stephanie live with it? Can she imagine her life without Morelli?

Because putting Morelli off while she explores her wilder side is a risky proposition. This is not a guy who will play second fiddle to anyone. He may be long gone by the time she gets her hormones in check. If I were in Stephanie's purple shoes, being older and hopefully somewhat wiser than I used to be, I'd settle on Morelli before one of the Terry Gilmans in his life decides to make a serious play. And when I say settle *on*, I don't mean settle *for*. Although descended from a long line of womanizing reprobates, Morelli is solid. Morelli is that rare combination of sexiness, toughness, and tenderness that's the stuff of women's dreams, which is why, for the most part, men like that are found only in romance fiction. Morelli may even be what has come to be rarer still—faithful—but the jury's still out on that one. Stephanie's life would be more of a mini-rollercoaster than the Cyclone, more on the edge than over the edge, but settling down with Morelli is hardly what I'd call settling.

However, I'm not Stephanie. There may be parallels in our experiences, but she displayed smarts and guts in dumping Dickie early on, and I have regrets. If I could do things over, I'd do them differently. Would I do a little bed-hopping? Probably. But even if I'd been born a couple of decades later I don't think flitting from bee to bee to bee is my style. I wouldn't, however, have married at twenty-two, and my experiences with a bee or two might have enabled me to differentiate among the Dickie Orrs, the Morellis, and the Rangers out there before making a lifelong commitment. So maybe Stephanie should go for it, take her chances and have her fling, so that she never has to look back with regret. On the other hand, looking at it from an author's perspective, she may need to keep up the balancing act at least until the fat lady sings and the series comes to an end, as all good things eventually must. Of course, I could suggest that Evanovich solve Stephanie's dilemma by knocking off one or the other of these guys, but that might precipitate a flood of book burning for which I wouldn't want to be responsible. Besides, I wouldn't have the temerity to suggest anything to Janet Evanovich. She needs no advice from me. Her fans love both these guys, and so do I. In Stephanie's larger-than-life Burb world they both have a place. My guess is, Stephanie will probably go on trying to have her cake and eat it too, and from time to time choking on it. But that's life—*c'est la vie*, as the French would say, or *c'est la guerre*, if that's where Stephanie takes us.

An aside: After my freshman year I transferred to an out-of-state school with an excellent drama department. I saw Charlie on and off over the next few years but the passion had dissipated. The magic was gone. I guess absence doesn't make the heart grow fonder, or maybe he wasn't my Morelli after all. When he graduated from college he joined the marines. The last time I saw him he was in uniform and carrying a swagger stick. The uniform was a turn-on, but for some reason I can't explain, the stick and the buzz cut put me off. Years later I met a mutual friend who told me she'd heard he'd become an Episcopal priest. Go figure.

Recently my sister mentioned to me that my brother had been fooling around since the tender age of twelve. I assume there were members of the female sex involved in these activities. So who were all those not-so-nice girls who were having so much more fun than his little sister, and how come they weren't branded for life?

As for my Dickie O., he married the tough and mean cookie he left me for, but once a cheat, always a cheat, and he cheated on her. Thirteen months after the big wedding they left on a trip to Australia. He didn't make it back alive.

I have an ironclad alibi.

NANCY TESLER was born in Worcester, Massachusetts, and received a Bachelor of Fine Arts from Carnegie Mellon University. After a career as an actor and a hiatus to raise three children, she began writing for the stage, TV, and the financial community. Her second career as a biofeedback clinician helped pay the bills when, single again, and inspired by the overwhelming urge to do someone in, she turned to writing murder mysteries. She is the author of five Carrie Carlin Other Deadly Things novels. She has just completed a stand-alone novel of romantic suspense and is currently working on the first of a new mystery series. Ms. Tesler lives in Tenafly, New Jersey.

THE FAST AND THE FURRY-OUS

WHY REX IS THE ONLY MAN STEPHANIE NEEDS

Rhonda Eudaly

Sometimes, when we're looking for the perfect man, we miss the one right under our noses....

Rex is pretty much nocturnal so we're sort of like ships passing in the night. As an extra treat, once in a while I drop a Cheez Doodle into his cage and he emerges from his soup-can home to retrieve the Doodle. That's about as complicated as our relationship gets.

—Stephanie Plum, *Eleven on Top* (6)

Complications. That is the keyword for Stephanie Plum's relationships with men, whether romantic, familial, or work-related. For a dozen books, we've watched Stephanie Plum ping pong between Ranger and Joe Morelli. Time and time again, when asked about her social life, she replies, "It's complicated." And it is—almost beyond comprehension. No one doubts she loves both men—and she's finally admitted the fact herself—but will she ever work through the complications to actually *choose* one? Doubtful. Steph sums it up pretty well in *Eleven on Top*: "They're both Mr. Right. And they're both Mr. Wrong....I wasn't sure I wanted a relationship with either of them. And I hadn't a clue how to choose between them" (4).

Well, here's a thought. *Don't!* Don't choose between them. And don't choose *either* of them. Why? Because if neither are Mr. Right, perhaps it's because there is already another guy in Stephanie's life, one who is being grievously overlooked in this equation. A better candidate than either of these fine gentlemen. I, of course, refer to Rex the Hamster. Yes, Rex the Hamster is the perfect man for Stephanie. Don't believe me? Let's look at the facts. And just the facts, ma'am.

Acceptance

Who is the only man in Stephanie's life who doesn't disapprove of her life as a bond enforcement agent? Rex. It's true. Rex is the only one who doesn't try to get Stephanie to change.

Joe Morelli's almost as bad as her *mother* about harping on how dangerous and unsuited Stephanie is as a bond enforcement agent. "'Other men have girlfriends with safe, normal jobs,' Morelli said. 'Like swallowing swords or getting shot out of a cannon.' And he hung up" (*Twelve Sharp* 186). And that's just on a normal day. Joe would like nothing more than for her to become some traditional housewife and stay out of trouble. He's said it. It's no secret.

At least he's not as vocal about it as her mother—and the less said *there* the better—but it's close. Though it could be argued that he does it out of a cop's concern for her safety. As he says to her in *Hard Eight*, "Cupcake, your *life* is scary" (78).

Which is true; even Steph will admit that. Let's face it, she's not a *good* bond enforcement agent—she's a *lucky* one. There is a difference and even she knows it. And as a testament to what she does admit to feeling for Morelli, she's thought about getting a different job...but staying at home all day wouldn't be our Stephanie.

Stephanie does give in to the pressure in *Eleven on Top* and quit her job at Vincent Plum Bail-Bonds (and that's enough mention of that sad excuse for a man). Look what that accomplishes. A whole lot of destruction and mayhem. The Burg will never be the same. Not that it's been the same to begin with, since Stephanie went to work for Vinnie. She will always be known as the one who burned down the funeral home, though it wasn't her fault.

Stephanie has three jobs in a week, experiences which include sexual harassment, a shoot out with a freaky old Italian lady with a legendary mole, two car bombs, and a grease fire. And where does she end up? Back working bond enforcement for Ranger! Morelli wonders if he has good insurance and calls Ranger a "poor, dumb bastard" for hiring her (190). Talk about your lack of support! Stephanie isn't cut out for the mundane, and she doesn't do nine to five. Even the supposedly boring computer job Ranger gave her turned into, not only overtime, but field work!

Ranger seems to accept her on the surface, but does he really? Or does he simply tolerate her because she's amusing to him? He's told Stephanie that she's a line item in his entertainment budget. Entertainment? What's that about?

He calls her "babe" nine times out of ten, and their relationship has generally been one of "double entendres and unresolved sexual tension. But we were also partners, of sorts..." (*Hard Eight* 52). Ranger is the type of mentor who tries to mold his student into an image of himself—at least professionally. He continuously tries to make her carry the gun she prefers to leave in the cookie jar. And for a while there, Ranger's help had a price—one night spent with him, doing whatever he wanted. That doesn't sound like a professional partnership to me—unless it's one along the lines of Lula's former occupation. In light of this amusement at her expense, can it really be said that he accepts her completely for who she is? I don't think so.

Besides, what's wrong with being a bond enforcement agent? It puts a soup can over her head and grapes in the refrigerator. What more can a girl ask for? Stephanie's lucky and healthy, at least when she's not being shot at or beaten up. Why not leave well enough alone? She's stronger and tougher than either man gives her credit for. They should know she's more capable than she seems and let her prove it by living her life and doing her job.

Only Rex doesn't complain about her job, even when the people barging in, psychopathic killers on the fire escape, and general chaos disrupts his life. He is the one who waits for her to come home, greeting her with a whisker twitch and a reassuring presence. Steph can't say the same about Joe or Ranger.

Only Rex has accepted Stephanie for who and what she is. Rex has been her anchor. He's been there throughout every firebomb, relationship misfire, stalker, and hired hit-man—not to mention the family freak outs and the odd Christmas visitor. (Now that Diesel guy had some potential, but he left when his job was done. Go figure.) Rex has always been there, and very little fazes him: "Rex was sleeping in his soup can and didn't show a lot of concern. Rex had seen me in my idiot phase before" (*Four to Score* 136).

Attractiveness

What else does Stephanie look for in a male? Looks, physical fitness, strength? Okay, so all the males in her life have that. Both Morelli and

Ranger have the sex appeal of a movie star on steroids. Every woman wants to be in Stephanie's shoes—or perhaps, more accurately, in her bed—when it comes to the physicality of her men. In her own words in *Hot Six*, "Two of the men on my list of desirables actually desire me back. The problem being that they both sort of scare the hell out of me" (vii).

Morelli has the history to go with the Italian good looks:

> When he was younger, mothers statewide warned their daughters about Joe Morelli. And when he was younger, daughters statewide didn't give a darn what their mothers told them. Morelli's features were more angular these days....So women watched and wondered what it would be like to be with Morelli. I knew, of course, what it was like to be with Morelli. Morelli was magic (*High Five* 45–46).

And then there's Ranger: "Ranger's Cuban-American. His features are Anglo, his eyes are Latino, his skin is the color of a mocha latte, and his body is 'as good as a body can get'" (*High Five* 21–22). Stephanie finds him amazing because he can refuse dessert. In fact, that's one of the things he would change about her if he could: her eating habits.

But come on, "Ranger" isn't even a real name. It's a truck, or a job in the army. (It's not, for example, a strong, majestic name like "Rex.") He may be good for the occasional roll in the cedar shavings, but long term? Nuh-uh. Mystery and danger have their place, don't get me wrong; that's all hot and sexy. But Stephanie has enough of that in her job. She doesn't need it in a relationship.

Now, Rex is physically fit. All that running on the wheel has left behind some stunning muscle tone under all that fur. Unlike Ranger, he's not a health nut where food is concerned. In that way, Rex is much like Morelli; he loves Pino's, and Friday night pot-roast with the Plums. He'll eat anything Stephanie gives him, from hamster chow to Cheez Doodles. Rex gladly shares the spoils of Stephanie's many dinners at home with her family.

Reliability

Let's also look at how confident Stephanie feels about the men in her life. Does Stephanie have full confidence in either Ranger or Morelli? No. She keeps things from them time and again. And they keep things from her—though they say it's for her own good. She rarely tells them the full truth until she has to, and that's usually not until there's a dire threat to her physical safety. Otherwise they might try to stop her from doing something they think is stupid but she knows is necessary. She ditches the boys at almost every turn—mostly by going out windows, until they catch on—until Ranger has to find her with a GPS or a little help from Tank or Hal. If Stephanie trusted them, why wouldn't she tell them everything? Wouldn't she ask for help up front?

Instead, Stephanie turns to the most tried-and-true man in her life: Rex. She has confided everything in him...and he may be a captive audience living in his glass aquarium, but he's also a fantastic listener. He's got big ears and expressive whiskers. He's been her sounding board for everything, and Stephanie has found sage wisdom in Rex's strong silence. Moreover, Rex doesn't judge her. Stephanie says as much in *Hard Eight*: "One of the good things about hamsters is that you can tell them anything. Hamsters are nonjudgmental as long as you feed them" (127). And that's Rex to a T.

And let's face it, who is the *only* male Stephanie would run into a burning building to save, with complete disregard for her own safety? Rex. In *Four to Score*, the second she sees the smoke coming out of her apartment, her first thought is for Rex. She would've walked through the flames to get to him. Fortunately, Mrs. Karwatt had a key to the apartment and got to him first. When Steven Soder is left on Stephanie's sofa in *Hard Eight*, infesting it with "death cooties" (186), whom does she go back inside for? Rex. She finds comfort in hugging his cage while waiting for the police—and Morelli—to arrive.

She can't say the same about Ranger or Morelli. In fact, one of the first times she saw Joe Morelli after their teenage encounter behind the éclair case, she ran him over in a car and broke his leg. And I can't think of any building, burning or otherwise, Ranger wouldn't be able to get himself out of (or into). Why would Stephanie bother?

Speaking of Ranger—it's hard to have full confidence in someone who is constantly out of touch or off on his own missions. She can call him in for favors *if he's around*, but, considering he bargained with her for the last favor, that's more of a last resort. She never knows if or when he's going to make a job a sexual encounter, and whether or not it will be cheating on Joe. That keeps her out on her own until she's so far in over her head the price of the favor doesn't matter.

And unlike the other two, Rex has also been her defender. The other two men have rescued her, but Rex has come directly to her defense. There's a distinct difference. When Rex was held hostage in *Three to Get Deadly* and threatened by an unknown gunmen with a syringe of heroin, what did he do? He bit the bad guy in the thumb so that the guy was distracted enough to let Stephanie do her job and take him down. And in that moment, Stephanie was more afraid for Rex than she was for herself, which made it possible for her to forget about her own safety long enough to do what had to be done. Rex, for his part, got out of the way so she could. Can that ever be said for Morelli or Ranger? I don't think so.

Joe and Ranger have been known to walk straight into the path of bullets to save Stephanie. And Joe is called in at the last moment in almost every book to clean up the mess. But he's rarely there in the beginning. Neither is Ranger. Both men are usually two steps behind Stephanie when push comes to shove. Ranger's GPS systems are found and left behind. Morelli is at the other end of a cell phone or police radio call. Even Lula, Valerie, and Sally Sweet are in on the excitement more often than Morelli and Ranger. The two men are always there to rescue her from danger, but only Rex has been there to defend her in the heat of the battle.

There's also the issue of availability. Only Rex has traveled with her from place to place. Neither Ranger nor Morelli have been around consistently.

The on-again/off-again nature of Morelli and Stephanie's relationship is due in part to this lack of availability. Morelli hasn't always been able to be there for her because of his job as a cop. He's constantly being taken away from her for work, as in *Visions of Sugar Plums* when he first meets Diesel. Morelli barely has time for a snide comment before his pager goes off. He's rarely around in *Twelve Sharp* because of gang war deaths. The only time he was consistently around was in *Eleven on Top*, but that's only because he was laid up with a broken leg from being run over (this time *not* by Stephanie), and in the end, couldn't even be there for the take down.

As for Ranger, his problem continues to be that he's a mercenary. He's dark and secretive which, alluring as that can be, plays havoc on stability. He helps her out when he's around, but that's the point—*when he's around*. There are several in which Ranger is either completely out of the picture, out of town on business, or *is* the business and Stephanie is trying to find *him*. He isn't consistent; stable isn't even in his vocabulary. She still doesn't know where his home is. (She's found his office and one of his apartments, but she realizes it's not his home.) She's never had to ask that about Rex.

Rex provides stability that even other people notice. She always knows where he is because he lives in a glass aquarium on the counter. Anyone's counter. She has taken him to Morelli's every single time she's lived with him. She takes him to Ranger's when she hides out at his apartment in *Ten Big Ones*. She finally admits while staying with Ranger to only *like* leaving Rex on his own for a couple of days. However, she has no problem leaving Ranger and Joe for longer when necessary. Stephanie needs Rex in ways she doesn't need Joe or Ranger. She relies on him to show her life is all as it should be. "The soft whir of his wheel reassured me that Rex was safe and there weren't any rock trolls hiding in my closet tonight" (*Visions of Sugar Plums* 110). That's a huge relief for her.

Nor does Rex require any admissions of love. That's one of the biggest complications of them all. Morelli has said the L-word to her, but she couldn't say it back for the longest time. She could feel it; she just couldn't say it. Ranger has admitted to loving her "in his own way." But come on, what does that mean? No one knows. Stephanie sure doesn't.

The final nail in the proverbial coffin—not that there haven't been literal coffins—is Christmas. In *Visions of Sugar Plums*, the only person in her life that Stephanie has planned a gift for? Rex. Granted her plan is to give him a raisin, but it's a plan! She runs through the mall on Christmas Eve for everyone else. And then in great Stephanie Plum fashion, all the Christmas presents are burned in an electrical fire initiated by John Ring. But that doesn't ruin her plan for Rex. Nor does he care; he loves his raisin. He's easy about things like that.

And therein lies the point. Stephanie needs easy. She needs uncomplicated. She has enough "complicated" in her life with her family and job. She doesn't need it in her man. Joe Morelli and Ranger are nothing but complicated. Rex is the One. The only man she'll ever need. Diesel said it best after having one dinner at the Plum House: "You were smart to choose the hamster" (*Visions of Sugar Plums* 52).

Now if only Stephanie would also realize it, Rex would be set.

RHONDA EUDALY lives in Fort Worth, Texas, where she's worked in offices, banking, radio, and education to support her writing and her cat, Dixon. She will soon be adding her fiancé, Jimmy, and his dog, Diamond, to her family. She likes to spend time with friends and family, swing dance, and read. Her two passions are writing and music.

Rhonda had more than a dozen fiction and non-fiction stories published in various anthologies, magazines, and Web sites. Check out her Web site—www.RhondaEudaly.com—for more information.

OTHER DISASTERS

THE GUN IN THE COOKIE JAR

A NONVIOLENT APPROACH
TO FUGITIVE APPREHENSION

Brenda Scott Royce

*Brenda Scott Royce's job is to separate what's really impor-
tant in a story from what's just window dressing—she's an
abridger for audiobooks, Janet Evanovich's included. And in
the process of cutting down the Stephanie Plum books, she's
discovered a secret: Under all of the jokes, the unorthodox
captures, and the apparently helpless flailing about, Stephanie's not nearly as bad at this whole bounty hunting gig as
we've been led to believe.*

LULA: What's the plan? We gonna just bust in like gangsta bounty
    hunters and kick his ass?
STEPHANIE: Have we *ever* done that?
LULA: Don't mean we can't.

                    —*Twelve Sharp* (11)

Stephanie Plum is not the world's best bounty hunter. And she's not
the worst. Or so Janet Evanovich tells the reader at the outset of nearly every installment of the Stephanie Plum mystery series.

Unlike the rough-and-tumble, rifle-toting bounty hunter of Western
flicks, Stephanie is rarely armed, preferring to keep her gun—a little
.38 Smith and Wesson Chief's Special—at home in her cookie jar. Her
stun gun tends to malfunction at critical moments, and her pepper
spray is invariably lost amidst the clutter in her purse. When all else
fails, she's been known to blast a bad guy with hair spray.

While stereotypical bounty hunters bust through doors with guns
drawn and muscles flexed, Stephanie gets winded chasing after bad
guys—her lack of physical prowess owing to an aversion to exercise

and a fondness for pastry products. Admittedly "pretty wimpy when it comes to actual butt-kicking" (*Seven Up* 6), she's not buff enough to single-handedly subdue most fugitives—unless they're drunk or disoriented, and even then something often goes awry. She flies by the seat of her pants, often not piecing together the puzzle until after she has stumbled into the villain's lair.

Plum is the first to admit her shortcomings. She likens herself to Elmer Fudd and Lucy Ricardo, and calls herself and pseudo-partner Lula "the Abbott and Costello of law enforcement" (*Ten Big Ones* 87). But her self-deprecating wit and surface ineptitude belie a surprisingly high rate of success—in *Eleven on Top* she boasts close to a 90 percent apprehension rate.

So how did a gun-fearing, out-of-shape, former lingerie buyer become one of Trenton's top bond enforcement agents? She initially took the job (blackmailing her cousin Vinnie into hiring her) because she needed money. She says she sticks with it because she doesn't have to wear pantyhose—and the bonds office is across the street from a bakery. But whether it's fate or a fluke, Stephanie has stumbled onto something she's good at. She would have us believe she gets by on "dumb luck," but there's much more to her than meets the eye.

Cut to the Chase

My name is Brenda Scott Royce and I'm an audiobook abridger. I'm the person who takes a full-length book and cuts it down to the requisite length for an audiobook—often eliminating more than half of the original text while striving to maintain the style, pacing, and integrity of the author's words.

If you're one of those purists who believe abridging books is a mortal sin, you might want to skip ahead to the next essay. You're entitled to your opinion. And you're in good company—the venerable Stephen King states simply in *On Writing* that abridged audiobooks are "the pits." Thankfully for me—and my landlord—many authors don't hold abridging in such low regard. They view an abridgment as an *adaptation* of a book—much like a screenplay—and an opportunity to introduce their work to a different segment of the book-buying public.

Janet Evanovich falls into the latter camp. I know because I've been abridging her books for eight years and even after I've hit the delete key on thousands of her words, she hasn't used her wealth and influence to have me hog-tied, bitch-slapped, or forced to wear a scarlet letter "A" in public. In fact, she has called me an "awesome abridger." (Who needs Stephen King?)

I've adapted all the Stephanie Plum books from *Four to Score* to *Twelve Sharp*, with a couple of the Full series (coauthored by Evanovich and Charlotte Hughes) thrown in for good measure.

Not surprisingly, the more I like a book, the harder it is to take my red pencil to it. On the first pass of a Stephanie Plum novel, I'll laugh out loud at a snappy exchange between Stephanie and Lula, or drop my jaw at one of Grandma Mazur's outrageous antics, and think to myself *"That's* gotta stay in." Days later, as I'm nearing my deadline and still a thousand words over my target word count, I'll reluctantly admit that the bit isn't crucial to the plot, and out it goes.

Mysteries are tough to abridge because typically each scene contains some piece of the puzzle that is necessary to advance the plot and solve the crime. The Plum novels are particularly difficult because they tend to be tightly plotted and fast-paced, with snappy dialogue and concise descriptions of characters and settings.

But rather than defend the audio publishing industry or describe its methodology, my aim in this essay is to share what I've learned from eviscerating Evanovich...um, I mean, lovingly distilling her brilliance into three-hour audio scripts.

And that's this: *Stephanie isn't the doofus she claims to be.*

She Has a Dream

Despite her assertions that she's not all that good at her job, in the end Stephanie Plum usually gets her man, or woman, as the case may be. On the surface, she may be untrained, uncoordinated, dysfunctional, and disorganized, but underneath she's a pretty smart cookie who simply relies on a completely different skill set than most people in her profession.

With her gun perennially at home in her cookie jar (where another fictional crime fighter, Jim Rockford, also kept his), the most effective weapons in Stephanie's bounty hunting arsenal are her brain and her mouth. By bringing in criminals without shedding blood (for the most part), she demonstrates superior reasoning and interpersonal skills. A true doofus wouldn't be so adept at diffusing dangerous situations and managing difficult people.

At times she comes off like the queen of klutz, but Stephanie's pratfalls are offset by a pragmatism that allows her to think on her feet even while falling flat on her face. In the process, she performs a service to the community, restoring harmony to the Burg and making the streets safer for gossip-mongering grandmothers, bored blue-collar workers, and transvestite rock singers.

She may even be a modern-day Martin Luther King, Jr.

Okay, so she's white, female, and her dream may be no loftier than to pay her rent and have enough left over for a Pino's pizza and a pair of kick-ass shoes. But like King, she believes in using nonviolent action to bring about a peaceful resolution to conflict. Whenever possible, Stephanie uses words rather than weapons to bring in a skip—much like Mahatma Gandhi sought to mediate conflict through open dialogue with his opponents (although she and Gandhi would have never seen eye-to-eye on the fasting thing). And like Mother Teresa, she reaches out to those in need, helping countless less fortunate souls who cross her path.

Then again, Stephanie is no saint. She has shot a few people, twice when her own life was threatened and once when the suspect, Emmanuel Lowe, crudely propositioned her and she blasted him in the little toe. But her motives were selfless ("I did it for women worldwide. It was a public service" [*Eleven on Top* 83]), and she only resorts to the use of force when all else fails.

Unlike the aforementioned icons of nonviolence, Stephanie's opposition to guns is more practical than philosophical. They give her the willies. In *Seven Up*, she admits, "Wave a gun under my nose and everything in my body turns to liquid" (96).

In *Hot Six*, Lula attempts to stun-gun fugitive Elwood Steiger but zaps Mooner instead. Steiger shrieks that Lula has killed Mooner. Lula complains, "Did you hear a gunshot? I don't think so. I don't even have a gun because Ms. Antiviolence here made me leave my gun in the car" (269).

Not comfortable kicking down doors or roughing up roustabouts, Stephanie relies on straightforward psychology. She typically takes a direct approach—knocking on the door, introducing herself as a bond enforcement agent, and politely asking the absconder to accompany her to the courthouse to reschedule. Of course, that rarely works. Most fugitives either brandish a weapon or bolt out the back door.

That's when Stephanie's creativity kicks in. Among her more successful techniques are false bravado, empty threats, blind persistence, mother henning, half-truths, and outright lies. The nature of her job is such that Stephanie rarely has time to premeditate her next move, but even when acting on impulse, she relies more on skill than luck. She intuitively understands that some fugitives just need a little finessing, while for others, no amount of sweet-talking will do. Her victories may appear accidental, but it's the artful application of these tactics that ultimately lead her to triumph.

False Bravado

In the opening of *High Five*, Stephanie likens her job to being a Barbie doll without underpants. Just as bare-bottomed Barbie looks perfectly tailored and coifed on the outside, Stephanie's tough talk in the face of murderous prizefighters, sociopathic funeral home directors, and maniacal mobsters is usually just a façade.

She brings her Jersey attitude to bear in her first adventure, *One for the Money*, in which Benito Ramirez terrorizes her with his cat-and-mouse games. When he confronts her in a parking lot, Stephanie brazenly tells the boxer, "You don't scare me, and you don't excite me" (228).

Staring down fanatical war-gamer Eddie Abruzzi in *Hard Eight*, Stephanie retains a calm, cool exterior despite her inner terror. While she boldly tells Abruzzi that his scare tactics don't impress her, she admits to herself, "I could feel every muscle in my body go into contraction. It was like I was squinting from my eyeballs clear down to my sphincter" (249).

Stephanie even keeps her cool when über-undertaker Constantine Stiva seals her in a coffin and threatens to hack her to pieces in *Eleven on Top*. Knowing that her best chance for survival is to stall for time, she keeps Con talking, barely breaking a sweat as she gets him to confess to a string of murders.

In *Seven Up*, after she persuades a pair of goombahs that she has mobster Louis DeStefano's heart on ice, Lula comments, "You were so freaking cool in there. You actually had me thinking you knew what you were doing" (207).

Empty Threats

Often used in tandem with false bravado, empty threats can be an effective way to gain an FTA's cooperation. In *One for the Money*, Stephanie has to bring in William Earling, a seventy-six-year-old flasher who lives in her apartment building. When he resists, she tells him, "Listen, Grandpa, either you go peaceably or I'll gas you and drag you out by your heels" (242). It's doubtful Stephanie would follow through on the threat, but the ploy works. The elderly exhibitionist not only agrees to accompany Stephanie to the courthouse, but also lets her borrow his car to bring him in.

Hard Eight opens with Stephanie trying to drag an overweight bail jumper, Martin Paulson, into the courthouse. He's in cuffs and leg shackles and keeps losing his balance. Stephanie asks Paulson if he's heard the bounty hunter slogan, "Bring 'em back, dead or alive." When he responds affirmatively, she deadpans, "Don't tempt me."

To the reader, she admits, "Actually, bringing someone back dead is a big no-no, but this seemed like a good time to make an empty threat. It was late afternoon. It was spring. And I wanted to get on with my life" (3).

Blind Persistence

Stephanie's tenacity in the face of death threats, car bombs, and greased-up naked fat guys is truly astounding. In *Two for the Dough*, Morelli tells her, "You've got the temperament of a pit bull with a soup bone when you're on a case" (16).

In *Eleven on Top*, she catalogues just a few of the pitfalls of her job: "I've been stalked by crazed killers, taunted by naked fat men, fire-bombed, shot at, spat at, cussed at, chased by humping dogs, attacked by a flock of Canadian honkers, rolled in garbage, and my cars get destroyed at an alarming rate" (4). But no matter what indignities she suffers at the hands of a slippery suspect, we know that she'll return again to try another day.

Stephanie spends most of *Hard Eight* trying to bring in Andy Bender, a drunk charged with domestic violence. Though he's constantly crocked, he manages to evade capture several times—once he even drives away in Stephanie's car while he's chained to it.

Then there's her pursuit of elderly Eddie DeChooch in *Seven Up*.

DeChooch, wanted for smuggling cigarettes, is depressed, nearly blind, and driving all over town in a big white Cadillac—but he keeps slipping through Stephanie's fingers. She tries to take him down when he's in church, sharing a bottle of wine with Father Carolli, but DeChooch fires a few rounds, destroying the baptismal font and a painting of the crucifixion.

After a record number of botched attempts to capture DeChooch, the mobster turns up bandaged and bloody on her doorstep. He's ready to turn himself in, but he's too embarrassed to be taken down by a girl. While she calls Ranger to make the actual apprehension, it's clearly Stephanie's collar.

Half-Truths and Outright Lies

According to Stephanie, her only real bounty hunter skill is her ability to fib. "I might be lacking a bunch of bounty hunter skills," she reflects in *Seven Up*, "but I can fib with the best of them" (48).

In *Two for the Dough*, she gains the cooperation of a fugitive's girlfriend by telling the woman that her boyfriend was cheating on her. She reasons, "I didn't feel bad about the lie, since Kenny was a scumbag felon, and Julia should be setting her sights higher anyway" (11).

In *Ten Big Ones*, she stretches the truth to get Sally Sweet off the hook for an assault charge, earning Lula's admiration. "Girl, you can lie! I almost gave myself a hemorrhoid trying not to laugh back there...It was inspired lying" (82).

Many of Stephanie's ploys rely on basic deception. She has posed as a delivery person, flashed a fake badge, and allowed people to be "temporarily confused" as to her law enforcement affiliation. In one outrageous scene, she picks up prostitute Roseanne Kreiner ("a businesswoman of the ho variety," in Connie's words [*Seven Up* 101]) by asking if Kreiner does women. The indiscriminating Kreiner says she'll do women, along with a variety of barnyard animals. Stephanie offers Kreiner a twenty, and when the hooker hops into the car, Steph hits the door locks and takes off toward the police station.

While she calls her standard line about coming to the courthouse to reschedule "a load of baloney," it's actually more of a half-truth. Stephanie just makes the chore sound like a minor inconvenience, like a trip to the post office. She fails to mention that, unless they are bonded back out immediately, the accused will then sit in lock-up until trial.

(Lying may be an asset to her job, but when dealing with her family, sometimes Stephanie has a hard time putting on the brakes. In *Eleven on Top*, her claims to play the cello hilariously backfire, while in *Seven Up*, her lies about setting a wedding date with Morelli keep escalating until her mother and grandmother have helped her pick out a wedding gown and reserve a reception hall.)

Mother Henning

While she doesn't consciously set out to be a mother hen to misfit miscreants, invariably Stephanie encounters a wayward bondee whose luck has turned sour, and her maternal instincts kick into overdrive. By lending a sympathetic ear and tending to their more pressing problems, she earns their gratitude—and often their cooperation. Some of these special cases go willingly to the courthouse, and a few turn up on her doorstep even after their legal woes are settled.

Stephanie's softer side causes Ranger to comment in *Hard Eight*, "You really should think about getting into a different line of work. Grooming kitty cats, maybe" (295).

Soft-hearted Stephanie goes to great lengths to accommodate some of these sad-sack FTAs. She practically adopts Randy Briggs, a diminutive computer programmer whose door she breaks down in *High Five*. When he's re-released, rather than return to a doorless apartment, he moves in with Stephanie—until he decides that even without a door, his place is safer than Stephanie's.

She talks Carol Zabo off a bridge in *Hot Six*. Carol shoplifted crotchless panties from Fredericks of Hollywood because she couldn't bring herself to pay for them. Stephanie calls in a favor with the arresting officer so Carol won't have to do jail time.

She is similarly solicitous of Sally Sweet, the transvestite musician who faces an assault charge in *Ten Big Ones*. Sweet drives a school bus during the day and missed his court date because he didn't want to take time off and let down the "little dudes." Stephanie promises to get him a court date during the middle of the day, between bus runs. She eventually strong-arms Sweet's accuser into dropping the charges.

When we first encounter Walter "Moon Man" Dunphy in *Hot Six*, he doesn't want to go to the courthouse with Stephanie because he's in the middle of a *Rocky & Bullwinkle* retrospective. Stephanie offers to go have lunch with her mother and return later. In *Seven Up*, Mooner moves in with her after he's shot by a vengeful mob widow.

In *Twelve Sharp*, Melvin Pickle is a mild-mannered shoe salesman who was caught masturbating in the multiplex. When Stephanie shows up at the shoe store, Pickle takes off running. She eventually catches up with him on the sixth-floor balcony of a neighboring hotel. Pickle, distraught over being "a pervert loser," threatens to jump.

Pickle laments, "My wife left me and took everything, including my clothes and my dog. I got fired from my job and had to go to work in a shoe store. I have no money, so I had to move back home and live with my mother. And I got caught whacking off in a multiplex. Could it possibly get any worse?"

Stephanie replies, "You have your health" (20).

She talks Pickle down by offering solutions to his most pressing problems. She even offers to get him a filing job at the bail bonds office. Morelli, who is listening in via cell phone, tells Stephanie, "Okay, so far we've promised him community service, vitamins, and a job. The only thing left that he could possibly want is gorilla sex. And if you promise that to him I'm not going to be happy" (22).

In the same book, Stephanie meets a woman after her own heart—menopausal Mary Lee Truk, who stabbed her husband in the butt. When Stephanie and Lula arrive, Mary Lee's in the middle of a hot flash and refuses to leave the house because her hair's a mess. Stephanie sticks a baseball cap over Mary Lee's head and brings the hormonal woman to the bakery, where she is soothed by the sight of rows upon rows of brightly colored doughnuts. Ah, the power of comfort food.

Quick Thinking

Stephanie's first big capture was Joe Morelli, who would become her on-again, off-again love interest throughout the series. In *One for the Money*, Morelli is wanted for killing an unarmed man. Stephanie isn't convinced he's guilty, but she's not convinced he's innocent either.

She's torn between helping him solve the murder and bringing him in and collecting her $10,000 fee.

After several bungled attempts to nab Morelli, she's pretty much resigned to letting him call the shots. But he pushes her one step too far, arrogantly announcing that she's incapable of capturing him without his cooperation. He's standing in a refrigerator truck as he makes this claim. Big mistake. Steph slams the freezer door shut and drives the truck straight to the police station.

When she's held at gunpoint by a mobster's schizophrenic widow and her sister in *Seven Up*, Stephanie acts on pure gut instinct. In a rush of adrenaline and blind fear, she lunges for the gun and manages to turn the tables on the sinister sisters, rescuing lovable losers Mooner and Dougie in the process.

A Little Help from Her Friends

And let's not forget, Stephanie has a gaggle of friends and relatives she calls on for advice and assistance. Having a cousin or high school chum who works at the DMV, phone company, or post office comes in handy when trying to track down a skip. Then there's Lula, Connie, Grandma Mazur, Stephanie's parents, her sister Valerie, Val's husband Albert Kloughn, and even Sally Sweet. From riding shotgun to sharing Burg gossip, performing computer searches or providing a place to park Rex for the night, Stephanie's motley crew comes to her aid in myriad ways.

And the two men in her life always have her back. Morelli has compromised his badge by bending police rules in order to save her skin. And it's presumed that Ranger kills a madman to protect her in *Hard Eight*.

Damn skippy.

She's Come a Long Way, Baby

Stephanie Plum is not the world's best bounty hunter. Nor is she the worst. She's neither a paragon of nonviolent virtue nor a blundering klutz. And she has evolved over the course of twelve books. In *One for the Money*, Stephanie clearly has no clue how to be a bounty hunter, but she is driven to do it for purely financial reasons. By *Eleven on*

Top, she's ready to throw in the towel. But disaster follows Steph as she works a succession of "regular" jobs and by *Twelve Sharp*, she's back in the bounty-hunting saddle again. This time, her tracking skills even impress her mentor, Ranger.

Yet even despite this growth, she still wears the mantle of the bumbling bounty hunter with an almost perverse pride, understating her abilities and attributing her successes to dumb luck.

She claims to have few discernible skills, but an examination of her techniques reveals this isn't true. She may not possess Morelli's street smarts or Ranger's seemingly superhuman abilities, but she's resourceful, resilient, and quick-witted. So why does she—and those around her—undervalue her abilities? Perhaps because a capable, competent, self-confident Plum would not be the endearing, lovable kook that readers—and audiobook listeners—have come to know and love.

If there's one thing I've learned from abridging the Plum books, it's that, even in truncated form, the essence of Stephanie—her deceptively ditzy, problem-plagued character—must shine through. You can shorten a family dinner, eliminate half the snappy dialogue between Stephanie and Lula, or delete a scene altogether if it doesn't advance the mystery plot. But you can't mess with Steph.

Part of Stephanie's massive appeal is her humanness. She's not Superwoman, but Everywoman. She's the girl next door—if the girl next door was having a really rotten day. She's an ordinary individual placed in extraordinary circumstances—the type of character fans can readily identify with, again and again and again.

In addition to condensing other people's novels, **BRENDA SCOTT ROYCE** has written one of her own—*Monkey Love*, which Janet Evanovich hailed as "Delicious as a jelly doughnut!" Like Stephanie Plum, Holly Heckerling, the plucky heroine of *Monkey Love*, juggles romantic entanglements, career disasters, and wacky relatives—but at least nobody shoots at her! (The most menacing character in *Monkey Love* is a mischievous monkey with a mad crush on Regis Philbin.) Not surprisingly, given her love of all things monkey, Brenda is Director of Publications for the Los Angeles Zoo. She has completed *Monkey Star*, the sequel to *Monkey Love*, and is contemplating more monkey adventures.

FROM DISASTER TO DIVA

WHY LULA SHOULD BE THE NEXT
SELF-HELP GODDESS

Natasha Fondren

Who knew, when we first met Lula in One for the Money, *that she'd become such an important part of the Stephanie Plum series? She's come a long way while still remaining wholly, unmistakably herself, from prostitute to office worker to bounty hunter in her own right (sort of). When you think about it, really, Lula's story is downright inspirational....*

THE IDEA POPPED IN MY MIND before I could stop it: Lula as self-help goddess.

Hah! I laughed at myself. *Surely not.*

Yet there the idea was, stuck in my head like a mosquito in a tent.

No, Lula? The 230-pound Lula? Goofy sidekick of Stephanie Plum? You mean, Lula the ho?

Yes! Yes, and yes. And no, she's not a prostitute anymore.

Believe it or not, I thought very little of Lula when I first read the adventures of Stephanie Plum. I loved watching the cars blow up and the coffins pop open—and Ranger. Boy, was I distracted by Ranger. I dreamed of Ranger, fantasized about Ranger, and fell in *love* with Ranger. I only noticed Lula when she drooled over Ranger (*that* was something I could identify with).

No, the idea of Lula as self-help goddess was something that came on gradually, after I worked past my Ranger-frenzy and discovered I had fallen in love with all the characters in the Stephanie Plum series—especially Lula.

Well, see, this is fiction, not another one of the self-help manuals that you collect...

Me? I don't collect self-help books, no.

A whole bookshelf filled with the things isn't a collection?

Just research. For this article, you see.

Uh-huh. And that's why you've got nearly every self-help book since I'm Okay, You're Okay *from the seventies?*

Well. . . .

Okay, it's true: I'm a self-help addict. Self-help books have been my friends and therapists through many a life crisis. When life gets stressful, I read a self-help book. When I get a little down, you can find me at Borders in the "Self Improvement" section. Last year I gained twenty pounds. What do you think I did? Workout? Curb my eating habits?

Hah! Of course not. Much easier to read a batch of diet books. So it was only this past summer, when I was having a bit of fall-doldrums-slash-career-crisis, that I made my way back towards the fix-your-life-in-ten-easy-steps shelves.

And tripped over a book.

Oh, come on . . . I don't believe that.

No! It's true!

Uh-huh, sure.

Well . . . it *was* sticking out of its shelf, and it did catch my eye, if not my foot.

Thought so.

So anyway, I noticed *One for the Money* sticking out. Who hasn't heard of Janet Evanovich? I'd seen her books, heard about her books, and even read the backs of a few. Something hooked me this time, and I finally bought it. Perhaps word of mouth had worn me down. Or maybe it was the fact that Stephanie was down on her luck and broke. I figured if she could turn her life around, then maybe I could learn something from this little, funny book.

Besides, being a bounty hunter may look fun and adventurous, but *come on*. What job doesn't look good when compared to Stephanie's daily brushes with death? What living abode doesn't look like heaven when compared with Stephanie's rinky-dink apartment, with strange men breaking in all the time? And how many of her cars have been blown up, already?

I never made it to the self-help section that day. In fact, I laughed so much reading the book that I plum forgot about getting my self-help fix. Underneath the layers of comedy in the Stephanie Plum series, I found kindred spirits—normal folk, in extraordinary circumstances, making the best of things, bettering themselves, and getting through the rocky times.

Sure, I dream about waking up as Sydney Bristow or Lara Croft and kicking some major ass in my perfectly toned body, but those are *dreams*. When Sydney throws a roundhouse kick, a bad guy goes down. When I attempt a roundhouse kick, *I* go down (for six months, no less...).

In my better fantasies, I pretend that I can wake up and be as kick-ass as Lara Croft, or live as colorfully as Mama Gena, or be as good a role model as Oprah. It came as a bit of a surprise to me that I found myself—during a particularly embarrassing moment—with the thought, "*Lula* wouldn't be embarrassed." It gave me comfort, so I soon discovered myself frequently wondering, "What would Lula do?"

You know she's not a real person, right?

But what is real?

What kind of nonsense question is that?

Well, in *The Velveteen Rabbit*, the Skin Horse says, "Real isn't how you are made.... It's a thing that happens to you. When a child loves you for a long, long time not just to play with, but REALLY loves you, then you become real" (Williams 5).

Whoa! That's a children's book, not a self-help book.

Take that up with Toni Raiten-D'Antonio, who wrote a book called *The Velveteen Principles*, which is a guide for adults—based on the lessons in the children's story—on, according to the front flap, "becoming *Real*—*Real* with yourself, *Real* with your hopes and desires...."

Humph, another one of your self-help manuals. So you're saying that you really love Lula, so she is real?

Well, no. I'm saying that I'm *really* inspired by Lula, so she is real enough.

Lula's story begins like most self-help gurus', with a down-on-her-luck story. Suze Orman, financial advisor, talks about her years of depression after a work disaster, when she lived off debt and more debt until she couldn't afford to pay a forty-dollar speeding ticket (Orman 3). Anthony Robbins describes his pre-enlightened self as "lonely, miserable, and thirty-eight pounds overweight....I was financially broke and emotionally bankrupt" (Robbins 22). Of course, both went on to riches and fame, preaching their way as the way for all of us to live happily ever after.

Lula's disaster story is more dramatic. We first meet Lula on the streets, working as a prostitute. She admirably shares with Stephanie all she knows about the "freak" Ramirez, even though the girl working the same corner warns her of the danger. "Nobody mess with Lula," Lula responds (*One for the Money* 195).

Unfortunately, Ramirez *does* mess with Lula, tying her to Stephanie's fire escape. He hangs her like a "big rag doll...naked and blood-smeared" (*One for the Money* 208). She's barely alive, and spends the remainder of the book in the hospital, fighting for her life.

Now that's a down-on-her-luck story!

Unlike Suze Orman, who goes from near-bankruptcy to financial perfection, or Anthony Robbins, who goes from flabby loser to mega-success man, Lula does not become annoyingly perfect.

What's so refreshing about Lula as self-help goddess is her *real*ness.

TV viewers watched Oprah struggle with her weight for years, losing it, then ballooning up again, in a frustrating cycle that we all could identify with—a cycle I can *definitely* identify with. *Real* people don't go from a problem-filled life to a life of perfect happiness in a snap. Oprah became a mentor and leader for women around the world, and a good part of her strength as a mentor is that she struggles to reach her goals, just like the rest of us.

In the Stephanie Plum series, we watch Lula's ups and downs with the same fascination. It's a relief that we're not the only ones who struggle. We're not the only ones who make mistakes. She takes a few steps forward, and then a couple steps back, and that's *real*. I can stuff my face with a chocolate doughnut and know that I'm not the only one in the world who falls off the wagon, now and then.

In spite of the setbacks and the obstacles, Lula digs her heels in and does what her friends are afraid to do, and no matter what happens, she gets up and keeps going. Lula isn't admirable because she's struggled and become perfect; she's admirable because she keeps pushing herself to grow and learn, day after mishap after day.

But she's fat!

Shhhh!!!!! Don't let her hear you say that.

And why not? It's true!

She'll squash you! She'll buzz you with her stun gun!

Uh, you remember? She's not a real person!

Whatever. And besides, *I'm* going to squash you if you make one more disparaging remark about being fat.

Fine, but why Lula? Why not Stephanie? Stephanie seems to be a lot more together than Lula....

In *How to Write*, Janet Evanovich says that "Lula is Stephanie times two" (19). Stephanie's down-on-her-luck story consists of losing her job as a lingerie buyer, whereas Lula's story contains a near-death disaster. Stephanie struggles with a few extra pounds; Lula attempts to lose more than sixty. When Stephanie trembles with fear, Lula either faints or takes off running, knees pumping high as she races from danger. If Stephanie is the *everywoman*, then Lula is double that.

With Lula, everything is amplified: her weight, her feelings, and her personality. Because her character is "Stephanie times two," the lessons we learn from her are also learned in a bigger way, and stick with us *because* of their outrageousness.

In his book *Shine*, Larry A. Thompson mentions the movie business adage, "Open big or you're dead!" (169). He goes on to explain that the saying tends to be true in life as well, specifically in our choice of style and dress.

With Lula, big is what you get. She dresses as she is: large, loud, and bold. She hides nothing when she dresses, not even her extra weight. Her favored pants are spandex—canary yellow and two sizes too small—in which she packs her extra pounds "solid. Bratwurst solid" (*Hot Six* 47). She may be a "substantial" woman, but no one calls her fat, at least not without getting squashed by said fat.

When she dresses, she puts herself out there, and there's a lot of personality for her to put out there. One wonders: if she didn't have those few extra pounds, where would all her personality go?

Throughout the series, she dyes her hair blonde, cherry, and even orange. Even without her spandex, she dresses in dazzling fashion. When she goes running with Ranger and Stephanie, she dresses all in pink, looking like the "Energizer rabbit on steroids" (*Three to Get Deadly* 231). Another time, she wears a hot-pink down ski jacket with white, fake-fur knee-high boots. And when she goes for the Wild West look, she goes all out, from the cowboy hat on her head all the way down to the ankle-length oiled canvas duster.

Stephanie sums up Lula's style with the following words: "On my own, on a good day with a ton of mascara and four-inch heels, I can attract some attention. Next to Lula I'm wallpaper" (*Seven Up* 8).

Lula's style says *here I am*. She flaunts her body with as little self-consciousness as she feels about her past. In *Ten Big Ones*, she says "I'm not ashamed of my past. I was a damn good ho" (91). She shows no shame for her life's journey, and she defends even her most questionable choices with pride. From the ghetto to the streets, and from a hospital bed to a respectable career, Lula never apologizes for her decisions, and her clothes show it. Lula dresses loudly, and never fails to make an impression—a *big* and *real* impression.

And she even faints with fear...
   What, you've never been afraid?
   Sydney Bristow and Lara Croft never get scared.
   Well, Sydney does, at least! Haven't you seen her trembling?
   Well, yeah, but—
   It's not brave if you're not scared.

Lula's style is not the only way in which she is Stephanie times two, nor is it the only way in which she lives her life grandly. When it comes to fear, we see, hear, and feel Lula's fear stronger than Stephanie's.

But fear times two does not mean that Lula is courageous by half.

Fear ignites our fight or flight instinct. Lula is no different. She ignores her fear either until it overcomes her, or until it indicates that she should flee. The inspiring trademark of Lula's fear is that she never fears her fear. Whether she acts with bravery or runs away, Lula faces her fears with the same boldness as she lives her life.

She often refuses to acknowledge her fear until it overwhelms her. Lula faints dead away when faced with Eddie Abruzzi—the ex-manager of Benito Ramirez, who almost killed her. When she comes to, she refuses to believe that she fainted, accusing her friends of lying to her. Up until she fainted, she stood her ground and looked her fear in the face. No one can blame her for succumbing to the living reminder of her torturous near-death confrontation with Ramirez. The fact that she faces his manager with her head held high and looks him in the eye is a lesson in courage.

Lula often does what Stephanie can't bring herself to do. In *Hard Eight*, Stephanie explains that "unjustified bravado" (127) is one of their trademark qualities, and Lula seems to demonstrate this trait the most. In reality, however, her bravado is more often true courage and a willingness to do what needs to be done rather than fake bravery.

Lula has a take-the-bull-by-the-horns approach to life. Even in the dangerous work they do, Lula isn't afraid to get the job done. When Stephanie needs to face her ex-husband to get important information on their case, Lula gets right to the business of *persuading* him to talk. She says, "Bet if I shoot him in the foot he tells us everything.... There's things I can do to a man. You'd probably throw up if I told you about them" (*Three to Get Deadly* 269).

In *Ten Big Ones*, Stephanie, Connie, and Lula bond out Anton Ward, a.k.a. Red Devil, in order to interrogate him. Even though Stephanie's life is at stake, Connie and Stephanie just don't have the courage to do what needs to be done. As usual, Lula steps up to the plate and shows us what courage is. When he doesn't talk, they give Lula a needle, and even though she squeezes her eyes shut and faints afterwards, she shoves that needle between his toes.

It's not brave if you're not scared.

Well, she's not much of a bounty hunter...

Do you realize how much Lula helped Stephanie develop into the bounty hunter she is today?

I'm not sure that's saying much. Stephanie's pretty lucky. Dumb lucky.

So she thinks. Look at how Lula helps and counsels her friends. Look at the example she sets and the advice she gives.

You make her sound like a mentor....

Unlike most self-help gurus, Lula doesn't write a book and preach her dogma to millions. In fact, Lula is too concerned about bettering herself and her friends to think about making money from strangers. She holds nothing back when telling her friends how to get what they want.

When Valerie needs to lose weight quickly before her wedding, Lula steps in and clears out Valerie's cupboards. Lula's an expert at losing weight—and unfortunately an expert at gaining it back, too. Refreshingly, Lula never sits on a high horse proclaiming the easy road to perfection. She nudges or shoves her friends towards their goals, and stays out of their way when necessary—like generously walking to the doughnut shop on her own, in order not to tempt her dieting friends.

In *Three to Get Deadly*, Lula counsels Stephanie on the importance of lying in order to get the truth out of someone. Stephanie becomes so good at fibbing—the first step in learning how to lie—that her mother asks her to play the cello for Valerie's wedding, even though Stephanie has never touched a cello. Stephanie's trademark luck saves her from having to own up to her fib, thanks to her car blowing up *again*—cello inside—and with fibbing mastered, Stephanie soon becomes an expert at all-out lying.

Like any mentor worth her salt, Lula holds nothing back when showering her students with praise. When Stephanie proves herself to be an accomplished liar, Lula doesn't just pat her on the back and say "good job." Lula praises in her over-the-top way, even *yelling*.

> "Girl, you can lie!" Lula yelled.... "You are the shit. I almost gave myself a hemorrhoid trying not to laugh back there. I can't believe how good you can lie. I mean, I've seen you lie before, but this was like Satan lying. It was inspired lying" (*Ten Big Ones* 61).

Lula advises her friends to play the role of what they aspire to be. She tells Pickle in *Twelve Sharp* that if he wants to be a pervert, he's got to learn not to blush. When Stephanie's Lincoln is riddled with bullets and decorated with gang graffiti, Lula encourages Stephanie to pick a role to play before she buckles under the fears and pressures of the contract out on her life. Stephanie decides to be smart and brave, and it works. By the next scene, she's calmly assessing her situation without falling apart.

Along with showing her fellow characters how to achieve their dreams, Lula sets an example. From going to night school to dieting, from becoming a bounty hunter to singing in a rock band, Lula embraces change and self-improvement in all that she does. She may change her goals, but she always goes after them with gusto, and encourages her friends to do the same.

And she's sure got a lot of weaknesses for a self-help goddess...

Weaknesses, shmeaknesses. Who's perfect? I'm not perfect.

No argument there.

Hey!

Well, that's why you're obsessed with self-help books. You're allowed to be human, but a self-help goddess?

Lula teaches us by example, and one of the greatest lessons she teaches us is how to turn our weaknesses into strengths. *Some* people would call a few extra pounds a weakness. (Not me! Not soft and cuddly me!) Her extra weight is part of what colors her character for readers, and she uses the weight to her advantage. Whether to protect herself or to capture and hold FTAs, Lula uses her poundage to physically squash her adversaries. She even goes so far as naming her technique the "Lula Bootie Bomb" (*Ten Big Ones* 202).

My personal favorite Lula weakness is the unabashed way in which she indulges herself. In one of my favorite self-help books, *Mama Gena's School of Womanly Arts*, Regena Thomashauer advises women on how to use the "power of pleasure" to create a "truly fulfilled life" (14). She teaches that self-indulgence is the key to self-empowerment and that our own pleasure not only makes us feel good, but infects those around us.

If anyone is a fine example of positive self-indulgence, it's Lula. First, there's the shoes and the shopping. When Lula feels down, she never sits and sulks. Lula acts, and she believes that there's nothing like new clothes or new shoes to make one feel better. Much like when she advocates playing a role to become whom you want, she buys clothes to look fabulous when she needs to feel fabulous. After Eddie Abruzzi scares her with the reminder of her trauma at the hands of Benito Ramirez, Lula goes out and buys a pair of kick-ass biker boots. A woman after my own heart!

When stress gets high—and it often does in their line of work— Lula's always the first one to suggest that they go get food. Lula knows that she and Stephanie can't save Trenton from the FTAs if they don't first see to their own needs and desires. (And Tastykakes are definitely an integral part of the road to happiness.)

And finally, Lula's not one to shy away from going after something she needs. When she becomes a full-fledged bounty hunter in *Eleven on Top*, she doesn't mind pausing in her duties to go after a man—even if he is an FTA. She may get handcuffed to the bed in the process, but when she sees a man she wants, she takes the opportunity to indulge her needs. She's not getting "it" regularly, she explains, and Willie Martin is a "fine" specimen of a man who once played pro football until he busted his knee (16).

Why would she resist indulging her fantasy?

In her own spectacular way, Lula sets an example of how to take care of ourselves and achieve our dreams. She turns her weaknesses—food, self-indulgence, shopping, and men—into assets that improve and spice up her life.

Fine, but face it, she's a disaster…

Disasters are a part of what make Lula *real*.

Now, let's not get into that argument again.

Okay, but disasters test characters more than anything else. Part of Lula's power as self-help goddess are her actions in the face of disasters.

During the ups and downs that tempt others to give up, Lula stays on course. When life throws her a disaster, she uses those disasters to see the good, not the bad.

Lula, despite tending to call things as she sees them, also looks at the bright side of things. When she's accused of being fat, she's quick to point out that she's "got none of that cellulite" (*Hot Six* 47). As she explained in *Four to Score*, "My glass is always half full. That's why I'm making something of myself" (119).

In *High Five*, Bunchy takes the wheels of Lula's new Firebird. Lula gets over her mad quickly, looking on the bright side. "Good thing I got auto club," she says. Even when Mrs. Nowicki flicks a cigarette butt under Stephanie's car and Lula's precious Firebird blows up too, she quickly moves past her outraged screeches into an "easy come, easy go" attitude. She starts to look forward to car shopping—her quest for healthy self-indulgence once more satisfied.

After Stephanie's Porsche, borrowed from Ranger, explodes itself and a neighboring garbage truck, Lula raves ecstatically about getting to watch a garbage truck blow up for the first time. And then when Stephanie's borrowed BMW gets stolen, she says, "Tell [Ranger] the good news is they left him his plates" (275).

Lula is quick to tell it like it is. "You got bad car karma," Lula says to Stephanie, but she's equally quick to mention the bright side: "But at least you're lucky at love" (*Ten Big Ones* 5). Even in her own life, Lula recalls her greatest disaster and worst trauma with a glass half-full philosophy. "I still got some pain from what Ramirez did to me, but turned out it was a favor. He stopped me from being a ho. When I got out of the hospital I knew I had to change my life" (*To the Nines* 73).

Amidst disasters, self-indulgence, and weaknesses, Lula shines through as a positive example of living life in the best way possible.

So Lula, self-help goddess?

Yes!

Lula teaches us to live *big*, to play the role we desire, and to look at life—the good and the bad—with a positive outlook. She may be a fictional character, but her *real*ness makes me believe self-improvement is possible, even during setbacks or disasters.

When I talk about the Stephanie Plum series, people invariably look off over my shoulder and mention Lula with a particularly fond smile. She is a character that people relate to and remember long after they've finished the latest book. When asked which character she would like to play if the series were made into a movie, Janet Evanovich chose Lula.

As Lula recommends, "We pick a role and we play it" (*Ten Big Ones* 223). I choose to play Lula, to live my life in a *big* and *real* way, mistakes, disasters, and all.

When she's not crushing on Ranger, **NATASHA FONDREN** keeps her fingers busy playing the roles of writer and pianist in Ohio. Thanks to Lula, she's learning to look on the bright side, even when disasters strike.

References

Evanovich, Janet with Ina Yalof. *How I Write: Secrets of a Bestselling Author*. New York: St. Martin's Griffin, 2006.

Orman, Suze. *The Courage to Be Rich*. New York: Riverhead Books, 2002.

Raiten-D'Antonio, Toni. *The Velveteen Principles*. Deerfield Beach: Health Communications, Inc., 2004.

Redman, Bridgette. "Janet Evanovich Talks on the Eve of Twelve Sharp." *Book Help Web*. June 2006. <http://www.bookhelpweb.com/authors/eva-onovich/interview.htm>

Robbins, Anthony. *Notes from a Friend: A Quick and Simple Guide to Taking Charge of Your Life*. New York: Fireside, 1995.

Thompson, Larry A. *Shine*. New York: McGraw-Hill, 2005.

Williams, Margery. *The Velveteen Rabbit*. New York: Doubleday, 1922.

STEPHANIE PLUM'S TRENTON

A GREAT PLACE FOR THE FAMILY?

Pam McCutcheon

The detective genre is known for having a strong sense of place, but Stephanie's hometown of Trenton, New Jersey, is a little more potent than most. The city, with all of its quirks and eccentricities—the smells, the sights, the drivers—comes alive in Evanovich's pages. So distinct is Stephanie's Trenton, in fact, that as far as those of us who've never been know, it might as well be the real thing....

PERSONAL AND CONFIDENTIAL

Report on the Feasibility of Expanding Mafia Operations
into Trenton, New Jersey

Boss, at your request, I have reviewed the possibility of expanding the Family's operations into Trenton, New Jersey. Since the airlines' tighter controls on hidden weaponry made it extremely difficult to visit the area safely in person, I sought out private accounts of residents in the belief that the people who live there know the area better than any casual visitor could glean in a few days. Luckily, the very information I needed fell off the back of a truck—a series of numbered diaries belonging to Trenton bounty hunter Stephanie Plum, as told to a woman named Janet Evanovich. After perusing them closely, I believe Ms. Plum's diaries provide exactly the information you need to make an informed decision. My observations follow.

Community/People

There are a number of residential areas in Trenton, but if you choose to relocate, the diaries indicate your best bet would be Chambersburg, known as "the Burg." Though houses are small and residents tend to hold on to them for life, it is possible to find (or make) occasional property available through death, marriage, or incarceration. In addition, the area is primarily Italian and Catholic, giving it that neighborly feel. The production of urea formaldehyde and the collection of offshore garbage in other parts of New Jersey gives the rest of Trenton a unique and unpleasant aroma, but the Burg is redolent of the scent of pizza (or tomato pie, as it is known locally).

The Burg has many retired capos and crew members, making the area very safe for families. Many Burg residents don't trust computers, banks, or the police, but are wise enough to go to a member of the Family down the street to get things done. Members of the Family who live in the area are careful to conduct operations elsewhere; everyone knows not to mess in their own backyard. Violators of this common-sense guideline have earned a one-way trip to the Camden landfill.

This part of the Garden State seems to have no gardens and cannot be considered at all attractive, but since it is as ugly as the rest of New Jersey, residents become used to it quickly. Though the houses and yards are small and narrow, they are neat and clean—obsessively so. Burg housewives are above reproach and are ready for company twenty-four hours a day, with refreshments available at all times (coffee cake is a staple). Windows are sparkling clean, the wash is white, and hearty meals are prompt and served at the same time every day. They don't worry about silly things like fat, sugar, or cholesterol in the Burg, and dinner is always followed by dessert.

The housewives attend mass regularly, keep a sharp eye on the neighborhood, and watch each other obsessively. Very little happens in this neighborhood without these women learning about it and sharing their knowledge with everyone they meet. However, if they see something they shouldn't, they also know when and how to keep their mouths shut. Burg women are great liars.

Residents of the Burg also have a fine appreciation of what constitutes traditional family values and girls are brought up with strong moral standards. They are taught the basics they need in life—applying make-up, styling hair, shopping, cooking, cleaning, and entertaining. In short, they learn everything they need to know to excel at being a good housewife, mother, and hostess. Though young women are taught early on that men don't buy the cow if they can get the milk for free, many of them still fall prey to our smooth-tongued Italian men who are naturally adept at talking women out of their panties and into playing "choo-choo." If Burg girls end up with a bun in the oven, their families ensure they do the right thing and marry the bum.

However, there are still many women in other parts of Trenton who are more than willing to put out for and put up with married Family men. Many will gladly endure abusive relationships to enjoy the prestige of being a mistress of the Mafia and the benefits of being with such rich, powerful, and successful men. Because both good and bad girls are in plentiful supply, this is an excellent place to keep our Young Turks entertained while they search for a proper Italian wife.

While Burg women take care of the houses, men take care of the cars (usually large) and spend hours in front of the most expensive television set they can afford. Residents are primarily blue collar and predominantly Italian (and proud of it). The activities of men in the Burg center around eating, drinking, cussing, slapping kids around, and cheating on their wives. However, most have the courtesy to do their philandering in a different town. As you can see, the Family would fit right in.

Extended families are common in the Burg, many living within five miles of each other. Though their lifestyle encourages obesity, diabetes, and heart disease, Burg residents who survive tend to live a long time, with an overabundance of senior citizens in the area. Many of them are colorful characters, providing hours of entertainment for their neighbors and mortification for their families. Embarrassing themselves and each other is not only accepted by Burg residents, it's expected. Luckily, no one thinks the worse of those who do so.

People in the Burg are unusually tolerant and adaptable. They don't blink an eye at seeing cars bombed, bodies sticking out of trunks (properly red flagged, of course), men disguised in masks and animal suits, and schizophrenics of all ages and nationalities packing heat to social functions. Even the school bus driver carries an Uzi, making your children's ride to school safe and homey. You couldn't ask for better neighbors.

Commerce

Trenton is primarily industrial. Historically, the city imported immigrants to work in the porcelain factories and steel mills, and contemporary businesses have continued that tradition with a number of factories employing blue-collar workers. Current plants include a button factory, a personal products factory (perfect to shake down to supply necessaries for the women in your life), a pork roll factory, a machine-tool factory, and numerous chemical factories. With the industrial atmosphere, a landfill in nearby Camden, and New York garbage being hauled off the Jersey shore, no one will question your waste management business cover.

From a close perusal of Ms. Plum's diaries, it appears other commerce in Trenton centers around food (including many grocery stores, bakeries, fast-food restaurants, and Italian eateries), used car lots, beauty parlors, bars, and small family owned businesses. Convenience seems to be a major factor in Trenton commerce with stores open every day of the week, including Sunday. The Quaker Bridge Mall nearby would provide ample shopping for your wife, daughter, and mistress.

With so many small Mom and Pop operations, opportunities abound for shakedowns and shylocking, especially with the lax security in most of the city. However, if you wanted to expand beyond your customary operations, there are some areas ripe for exploitation:

1. *Home repair/construction.* Breaking down doors and setting fires is common in Trenton. You could really clean up with a business providing substandard home construction materials at premium prices.
2. *Auto repair.* Trenton drivers are reckless and the accident rate is incredibly high. Though the frequent car bombings usually destroy the vehicles they hit, many others are damaged in the normal course of a day. A repair shop would provide much-needed services while allowing you to jack up the price of parts and labor to meet demand. And, of course, it would be the perfect front for a chop shop to supply inexpensive spare parts while making a much-needed source of used cars available to the Trenton community.
3. *Gun shop.* There are many gun owners in Trenton and most of

them use ammunition at an unusually high rate. They have to buy their ammunition and weapons somewhere. Why not from you? Imagine the potential for future gunrunning ventures. Other popular Trenton weapons you might want to stock are pepper spray, stun guns, and tasers. You could also do a brisk business in handcuffs, since bounty hunters seem to lose them frequently.

4. *Funeral services.* There are several mortuaries in the Trenton area, but the proprietor of the most popular one (Stiva's Mortuary) was recently arrested for illegally adding to his own customer base. Since management was taken over by a male couple ignorant of the business, gaining control would be easy. The building has been freshly renovated due to a fire and, with a new funeral director as a front, the mortuary could provide your Family with cut-rate funeral services, offer a legitimate excuse to have bodies on the premises, and have the added benefit of providing your mother with hours of entertainment while participating in the city's primary form of night life.

5. *Hazardous waste disposal.* Pollution in Trenton is common and expected; there are no tree-hugging environmentalists to protest the illegal dumping of toxic wastes, so this area is a potential gold mine. To avoid the EPA and its bothersome regulations, you could offload collected waste in abandoned factories, or if you have no objection to night operations, you could haul massive amounts to the Camden landfill and bury it under other garbage with no one the wiser. Changing the labels on the containers would be easy and ensure they wouldn't be traced back to you if they were found.

6. *Protection racket.* Though there are some small-time protection rackets operating in Trenton, the presence of so many small businesses whose proprietors can be intimidated leaves this field wide open and primed for development. And, since an inordinate number of threats seem to be made against pets (especially dogs and hamsters), you might consider expanding your operation to include these areas. It would be a perfect way to ease your teenaged son into the Family business.

7. *Pornography.* Porn is oddly lacking and underutilized in Trenton, though the men there make ideal customers for this form

of free enterprise. The arrest of a local candy store owner who created and distributed kiddie porn left a vacuum in an already sparse pornography business that is ready to be filled by our enterprising members. This gives the added advantage of being able to employ a pool of talented and attractive women that capos can troll for potential girlfriends.

Competition

There are some Family members currently in the area. The only made men in Trenton are retired and the others are low-level soldiers who work for Anthony "Thumbs" Thumbelli. I'm sure an arrangement could be made to take over his territory and give him a small taste of the action. If you have to "go to the mattresses" to establish your rightful dominance, there is very little risk. The soldiers in Trenton are incompetent and provide more amusement than grief to the local police.

A number of independent entrepreneurs in Trenton have bookmaking operations, operate protection rackets (as mentioned above), bootleg untaxed cigarettes, and sell materials that fell off the back of a truck, but they're small potatoes. In fact, they keep the Trenton Police Department busy and distracted with penny ante crime so the cops won't be looking in your direction.

The inner city area around Stark Street and Compton Street consists of bars, crack houses, substandard housing, hookers, and gangs. The gangs (Comstock Street Slayers, Crud and Guts, and the Cuts) predominate there, specializing in theft, drugs, prostitution, and murder. They would appear to be our primary competition. However, since one of the gangs uses powder blue as its color and another uses kitty cat paw prints as their mark, I doubt this bunch of *finooks* are any threat. In fact, the residents of Trenton fear the IRS more than the gangs.

Since these unorganized and inefficient gangs have a strong sense of territory, we can probably persuade them to confine their dealings to a few blocks. Or, if necessary, by dropping a few judicious lies in the right ears and flashing the wrong color or spraying graffiti in the wrong place, we can probably initiate a gang war and let them destroy each other.

Natural selection is also very much in play in Trenton. Incompetent *jamooks* are often taken out or become a guest of the state after coming up against the Trenton PD or bond enforcement officials from the Vincent Plum Bail Bonding Company.

Entertainment

Entertainment in Trenton and the Burg centers around food, gossip, and the local funeral parlors. People in the Burg know how to pay their respects to the dead. It doesn't matter what's going on in their own lives or if a warrant is out for their arrest, everyone pays proper respects at memorial services, even when the dearly departed is completely unknown to them. The Knights of Columbus and the Elks put on an excellent show while the mortuaries put out a good spread.

The local Trenton social clubs used to be active running numbers operations until New Jersey legalized gambling. Now they are primarily populated by senior citizens who reminisce about the good old days. However, Atlantic City and the shore are within close driving distance for those who feel the need to gamble at casinos or to make fools of themselves outside their home stomping grounds.

But there is no need to leave the city since there is a great deal of inexpensive entertainment available in Trenton. Male members of the Family will enjoy the bars and strip clubs, and women will enjoy the nearby mall, multiplex theater, and gossip at the beauty and funeral parlors. You needn't worry about snooty high-brows looking down on you; there aren't any in Trenton.

Public Services

An analysis of Trenton's public services follows:

1. *Traffic management.* Traffic in Trenton is heavy and the drivers are aggressive, so the Family should fit right in. Speed limits are routinely ignored and driving is a thrilling contact sport, with participants using traditional Italian hand gestures to communicate with each other. Parking is difficult and handicapped slots are highly prized commodities, with residents not above maiming themselves to obtain access to these coveted spaces.

2. *Fire department.* The fire department is exactly what we need. They are rarely in time to stop a fire from destroying its target, but usually keep it from spreading to other buildings. Fire prevention seems nonexistent.

3. *Medical care.* The city boasts three hospitals, the most popular being St. Francis. The personnel are discreet, making this hospital ideal for patching up wounded soldiers when you have an altercation or need to teach a lesson to a straying Family member.

4. *Burial.* Should injuries become fatal, five funeral homes do a booming business in Trenton and comprise a big part of the social life. See notes under COMMERCE for a possible business opportunity.

   In addition, nearby Camden, New Jersey, enjoys the reputation of being the most dangerous city its size in America (Trenton is fourth). The previously mentioned Camden landfill is conveniently located for all your disposal needs, and has been the final resting place of many an enemy of the Family.

5. *Law enforcement.* The Trenton Police Department is surrounded by the ghetto, where most of their business is transacted. Luckily for us, the Trenton cops are overworked and underpaid, with low budgets, long hours, and inadequate transportation. They are unlikely to interfere with your business.

6. *Bail bonding.* Inevitably, some Family members will be arrested and incarcerated. If that happens, there are several bail bond companies available to release them so you needn't risk your own assets. Gold Star Bail Bonds seems to be the best and has a properly respectful attitude for the apprehension process. Avoid Vincent Plum's Bail Bonding Company at all costs. Their bounty hunters not only have a high success rate in finding bail jumpers, but they seem more likely than most to use deceit, trickery, and weaponry when apprehending them. Humiliation and unfortunate accidents accompany many of their takedowns, especially those made by Stephanie Plum a.k.a. Babe a.k.a. Cupcake and her unofficial partner, Lula, a spandex-clad former *puttana* who is as dangerous as a loose cannon.

7. *Legal services.* Legal advice in Trenton is severely limited. Law firms consist primarily of incompetent wife-cheaters, and ambulance chasers who reside in Laundromats (two, oddly enough, are related to Ms. Plum). If you choose to relocate here, I suggest you import your own legal counsel.

8. *Court system.* Because the police and the courts are so overworked, common sense often supersedes written law in Tren-

ton. Residents understand that perjury is often the best way to ensure a long life and avoid permanent residence at the bottom of the Camden landfill.

9. *Prisons*. Though Ms. Plum's diaries neglect to mention it, for those few who are convicted by the courts, an Internet search shows that the New Jersey State Prison is conveniently located in Trenton, housing the state's most dangerous criminals along with two maximum security units. Since our compatriots are likely to be housed here, the convenient location makes it easy to visit those who have temporarily become guests of the state and, indeed, to continue conducting business even from their jail cells.

Conclusion

Though Ms. Plum's diaries would lead me to believe that Trenton would be an ideal location to expand your operation, I caution you to consider it carefully. Ms. Plum's personal accounts paint her as somewhat incompetent (and, in the case of two slim unnumbered volumes, prone to hallucinogenic visions apparently brought on by an overdose of sweets). However, these diaries may be a clever cover designed to disguise just how effective she really is. Her fugitive apprehension success rate is extremely high and though her belongings (especially her vehicles) take a lot of abuse, personal damage slides right off her, almost as if she's made of Teflon®. This points to either undue modesty on Ms. Plum's part in her diaries...or an extremely clever deception designed to lure us into the trap of complacency.

If she is as incompetent as she would have us believe, then her tenacity in pursuing hardened criminals despite her clear lack of ability would appear to be the act of a deranged mind. Either that, or she has more lives than a cat and enough luck for twenty people. However, no matter whether she is concealing her true abilities, is truly mad, or is simply very lucky, her presence in Trenton constitutes a significant danger to Family operations.

My initial thought was to suggest you put out a contract on her before expanding into the area, but her track record in eluding or foiling would-be assassins is unparalleled. In addition, she has the unprecedented backup of the community, the police (she has relatives, as well as an on-again, off-again boyfriend, Joe Morelli, on the force), and local security consultants, especially the frighteningly competent Ricardo Carlos "Ranger" Mañoso and his crew. I fear that trying to eliminate her would cost you too much manpower and result in undue humiliation to all concerned. Therefore, despite the undoubted allure of Trenton, I recommend you consider moving to Newark or Camden instead.

PAM McCUTCHEON grew up in Arizona and, though she traveled around the world as an engineer for the U.S. Air Force, she never made it to Trenton. Everything she does and doesn't know about Trenton and New Jersey she learned from Stephanie Plum and her talented creator, Janet Evanovich. Pam has published romantic comedy novels, fantasy short stories (under the name Pamela Luzier), and nonfiction books for writers. She lives in the mountains of Colorado with her dog, Mo, and has no plans ever to visit Trenton.

COULD STEPHANIE PLUM REALLY GET CAR INSURANCE?

JA Konrath

The Stephanie Plum books are fiction. No real woman, for instance, could eat like Stephanie does and still be able to fasten her jeans. But mostly, we know the books aren't real because, despite enough crashes, explosions, and other mishaps to overload a baker's dozen, there's someone out there still willing to give Stephanie Plum auto insurance.

By MY COUNT, Stephanie Plum has been involved in the loss or destruction of twelve vehicles at the time of this writing (8:55 A.M., Eastern Standard). But, in all fairness, I'm not very good at counting. Plus, I listened to two of the books on abridged audio, which is known for cutting incidental bits from novels, such as characterization and plot.

Since I had nothing better to do today, other than to donate my kidney to that sick guy who paid me fifty thousand dollars, I decided to find out if Ms. Plum could, in the real world, get insured.

Let's take a moment to look at the phrase "in the real world."

Have you taken a moment? Good. Let's move on.

Since Stephanie Plum is a fictitious character, who lives in a fictitious place called Trenton, New Jersey, she isn't expected to conform completely to all aspects of reality, such as car insurance, or gravity. But today's reader demands verisimilitude. (And I wish she'd stop demanding that, because it's rude to stomp around, demanding things. Plus, I'm not sure what *verisimilitude* means.)

Since I knew that the task before me would involve a great deal of painstaking research and determination, I immediately went to work. After work, I went to a movie. Then, I took a nap. I had to take the phone off the hook while I did it, too, because I kept getting obnoxious messages along the lines of "Where's that kidney?" and "You have to get to the hospital immediately!" and "He's dead."

Discouraged by my lack of progress, I plugged the phone back in and I called my neighbor Smitty, who knows a lot of stuff, such as why bottled water costs the same as bottled iced tea, even though it doesn't have all the stuff in it that tea has. Such as tea. And riboflavin. Quote Smitty:

"Stephanie who?"

So I pulled out my trusty phone book and began calling insurance companies. After eight calls that went nowhere, I decided I needed a better plan than giggling and making fart sounds into the phone when someone answered. So I tried talking.

Here are some of the conversations I had. My name has been changed to protect me.

CALL NUMBER ONE

ME: Do you sell car insurance?

INSURANCE MAN #1: Yes.

ME: My name is Julie Pear, and I'm not a fictitious character. I played a hand in destroying twelve cars in my last thirteen books. Will you insure me?

INSURANCE MAN #1: I need more information.

ME: I like the color red, and dogs.

INSURANCE MAN #1: I meant about your driving background.

ME: I also like Rob Schneider movies.

INSURANCE MAN #1: I'm sorry, we can't insure you.

CALL NUMBER TWO

ME: Hello?

INSURANCE MAN #2: Can I help you?

ME: My last four cars have exploded, but it wasn't my fault. Can you insure me?

INSURANCE MAN #2: How did these cars explode?

ME: I can't remember. I loaned the books to my Mom. Plus, I've been drinking.

INSURANCE MAN #2: Oh. Well, you're welcome to come in and we can give you a quote.

ME: How about I give you a quote instead? How about, "This was no boating accident!"

INSURANCE MAN #2: Excuse me?

ME: That was from *Jaws*. I loved that movie. I still get scared taking baths.

INSURANCE MAN #2: You're an idiot.

CALL NUMBER THREE

INSURANCE MAN #3: Making rude noises like that is very immature. (pause) I know you're still there, I can hear you giggling.

CALL NUMBER FOUR

ME: I want a large thin crust, sausage, and extra cheese.
PIZZA GUY: That will be $14.95.

But none of this tremendous effort brought me any closer to the end of this essay.

Undaunted, superfluous, and proselytical, I decided to try a more direct approach. Because even though I'm a writer, I've always wanted to direct.

So I wrote an impassioned, persuasive letter to the largest auto insurer next to my house. The letter brilliantly detailed the whole sordid tale, and was perhaps the greatest thing I've ever written on a cocktail napkin. Without permission, here is the company's reply:

```
                                    We Care Auto Insurance
                                   WE INSURE EVERYONE!™

                                        8866 Haknort Lane
                                        CHICAGO, IL 60610
                                         (847) 555 - AUTO
                            JACK@WECAREAUTOINSURANCE.COM
                                    www.AUTOINSURANCE.com

To: Margaret Apples
Re: Recent Insurance Inquiry

Ms. Apples—

When my father began We Care Auto Insurance sixty-four years
ago, he had a grand dream: supply auto insurance to everyone who
needed it, regardless of their driving record or accident his-
tory. He wanted to be the insurance company for the common man—
the senior citizens with senility issues, the veterans missing
important limbs, the narcoleptics, the mentally retarded, the
unrepentant alcoholics.
    Father believed everyone—even those with heroin habits and
cataracts the size of dinner plates—deserved to be insured. For
more than six decades, We Care Auto Insurance carried on this
proud tradition.
    We have insured drivers with organic brain damage of such
```

severity they couldn't count past four. We have insured drivers with quadriplegia, who drove using a suck-and-blow straw. We have insured the legally blind, the morbidly obese, the legally dead, and Mr. Chimpo the Driving Baboon. We've even insured several Kennedys.

Now, for the first time in our history, We Care Auto Insurance must turn down an application. Yours.

While the law doesn't require us to provide an explanation for the reason you aren't being allowed into the We Care Auto Insurance family, I've chosen to write this letter to make something perfectly clear: We are not to blame, Ms. Apples. You are.

While reviewing insurance applications, we compile statistics from several sources, which allow us to come up with monthly rates and deductible figures. When feeding your information into our computer database, our network promptly froze.

We haven't been able to reboot it.

According to the detailed information on that KFC napkin you sent us, you've been responsible for destroying more cars than any single driver in North America, and possibly South America as well.

You've destroyed more cars than Carzilla, the giant robotic crane that tours with monster truck shows and eats cars.

In layperson's terms: you've destroyed a huge fucking buttload of cars.

Allow me to reiterate:

After your Miata was repossessed (which seems to be the only nice car you've ever owned), you played a hand in the explosion of a Jeep owned by a Detective Gepetto of the Trenton Police Department. This, unfortunately, was not the last automobile casualty Detective Gepetto suffered at your hands.

Your next vehicle, a Jeep, was stolen. You'll be pleased to know that a VIN search has recently located it, in a scrap yard in Muncie, Indiana. The odometer reading was well over 220,000 miles. Having escaped you, this Jeep led a full and possibly interesting life, without explosions, though your insurance company still had to foot the bill for it nonetheless.

The blue Nissan truck you acquired shortly thereafter soon went to the big parking lot in the sky after being blown up with a rocket launcher. I must admit, I had to read the claim report three times before the phrase rocket launcher sunk in. I've insured several CIA operatives, a movie stuntman named Jimmy Rocket who specialized in pyrotechnics, and a scientist who actually worked for a rocket company (I believe they called him a rocket scientist), but none of them ever lost a vehicle to a rocket, missile, or any comparable exploding projectile.

Your replacement car, a Honda CRX, was soaked in gasoline and burned. My record search was unable to turn up the name of the perpetrator, but might I suggest it was one of your previous insurance agents? That wouldn't surprise me.

Your name came up in several claims made by a company cryptically called Sexy Cuban Man. The claims included an exploded Porsche and a stolen BMW. Not content with that, you somehow also managed to burn down a funeral home. Did you get confused in the dark and mistake it for a car somehow?

A Honda Civic, registered to you, was torched, and a Honda CRV registered to you was totaled, and then set ablaze. Why you bought another Honda is beyond my mental capacity, but you did, and it was promptly burned, along with another Sexy Cuban Man vehicle, by—and this is in your own words—a giant rabbit. Was Jimmy Stewart anywhere in the vicinity, pray tell? Or did this rabbit happen to have a basket of brightly colored eggs?

Your next vehicle, a Ford Escape, didn't escape at all. Again, it was burned. Perhaps car insurance isn't what you need. Perhaps you simply need a car made of asbestos. Or a Sherman Tank.

Your next victim, a Saturn, was bombed. So was an SUV belonging to the unfortunate Detective Gepetto. You also had a hand in the recent explosion of a Ford Escalade.

Records show you just purchased a Mini Cooper. Such an adorable car. I've included it in my nightly prayers.

While the first few explosions might be written off as coincidence, or even bad luck, somewhere around the tenth destroyed vehicle a little light came on inside my head. I finally understood that no one could be this unlucky. There was only one possible explanation.

You're sick in the head.

The psychiatric community calls your specific mental illness "Munchausen's by Proxy." A parent, usually the mother, purposely makes her children sick so she can bask in the attention and sympathy of others.

I've decided that this is what you're doing, only with vehicles. Rather than feeding little Molly peanut-butter-and-bleach-sandwiches, you've been deliberately destroying your own cars. All because you crave attention.

But your warped scheme to put the spotlight upon yourself isn't without casualties. I'm not speaking of your helpless automotive victims. I'm speaking of my company.

Writing this letter fills me with sadness, Ms. Apples, for you have destroyed my father's dream. For the first time in our history, we are rejecting an applicant. This comes at a great moral cost, and a great financial one as well.

Because of you, we have been forced to change our trademarked slogan, We Insure Everyone! Do you have any idea how much letterhead we have with that slogan on it? A warehouse full. And unless we hire someone (perhaps an immigrant, or a homeless person) to cross out the slogan on each individual sheet of paper, it is now land-fill bound.

Ditto our business cards. Our refrigerator magnets. Our full color calendars we give to our loyal customers every holiday season. The large and numerous interstate billboards. And our catchy TV commercials, which feature the jingle written by none other than Mr. Paul Williams, naturally called "We Insure Everyone."

What will our new slogan be? I'm not sure. There are several in the running. They include: "We Insure Practically Everyone," "We Really Want to Insure Everyone," and "We Insure Everyone But Margaret Apples." I also like the slogan "Why Can't You Be in the Next Car You Blow Up or at the Very Least Get a Job at the Button Factory," but that has too many words to fit on a business card.

You have crippled us, Ms. Apples. Crippled us worse than many of the people we insure, including the guy with the prosthetic pelvis and the woman born without arms who must steer with her face.

I hope you're happy.

As a public service to the world, I'm sending copies of this letter to every insurance agent in the United States. Hopefully, this will end your reign of terror.

If it takes every cent of my money, every single one of my vast resources, I'll see to it that you are never able to insure another vehicle again. When I get done with you, you won't be able to put on roller skates without the Feds breathing down your neck.

Whew. There. I feel a lot better now.

And though we aren't able to insure you, Ms. Apples, I do hope you pass our name along to any friends or relatives of yours who are seeking auto insurance.

Sincerely,

Milton McGlade

So there you have it. Based on the minutes of hard work I've devoted to this topic, Stephanie Plum would not be able to get car insurance.

In conclusion, if I had only ten words to end this essay, I'd have a really hard time thinking of them. Now if you'll excuse me, I've got a kidney to sell on eBay.

JA KONRATH writes the pretty funny Lt. Jacqueline "Jack" Daniels mystery series. *Whiskey Sour*, *Bloody Mary*, and *Rusty Nail* are currently in print, with threats of more coming soon.

THE STEPHANIE PLUM DIET

HOW TO HAVE A GREAT LIFE BY EATING FOOD YOU LOVE AND EXERCISING AS IF YOUR LIFE DEPENDED ON IT

Charlene Brusso

Maybe I spoke too soon about Stephanie's eating habits. It's important to remember, after all, that Stephanie's a lot more active than those of us who ride our desks all day. She's naturally going to need more calories. Charlene Brusso has some suggestions for how we, too, can be more like Stephanie and reap the benefits of her diet. The important part, Charlene says, is balance....

YOU KNOW THE FEELING: your seat belt's too tight, walking up a flight of stairs makes your breath heave and your heart race, your arch-nemesis called you a cow, and, worst of all, only the ugly clothes in your closet fit. You know you need to do it. You need to take control: you need to diet.

Believe it or not, you've just taken the first step toward a new life—a life that's simpler, healthier, and happier. Great bodies and high self-esteem don't come easily in today's fast-paced world of high-stress jobs, demanding relatives, and yo-yo romances. Fortunately, with the Stephanie Plum diet you can achieve your goals without committing yourself to harsh regimens of tasteless foods and unending visits to the health club. It's all about balancing body chemistry—those pesky carbohydrates, protein, fats, and sugars—with your all-too-typical break-neck lifestyle.

The Stephanie Plum Diet Triangle

You don't have to be a bounty hunter to have an erratic lifestyle and an even more chaotic meal schedule. You may not be able to control

147

life's daily demands, but you can make sure you have the energy to deal with them, even on a diet. That's what this plan is all about.

You've heard of romantic triangles. Well, think of this plan as an equilateral diet triangle. Each side represents a different feature of the plan. Each side is also the same size, re-enforcing the fact that each feature is equally important in making the diet work. The three sides are, in no particular order: Food, Exercise, and Attitude. That's all you need to know. Really. Forget counting calories and meal points. Forget sweaty workouts at so-called health clubs and canned "exercise" programs on video or DVD. Just remember the triangle, and success is certain.

The three sides of our diet triangle all have something else in common besides size, and that something is *flexibility*. With this plan you can look forward to never having to eat the same old meal or perform the same old exercise twice in a row. Eating a wide range of foods and breaking up periods of strenuous activity with relaxing zone-outs in front of the tube will keep you from falling into dangerously boring, repetitive patterns.

Stick with this diet and you won't just find your ideal weight. You'll also learn a lot about yourself, your family, your friends—and your enemies. And isn't discovery what life is all about?

Food

Everyone, from lingerie buyers to superheroes, needs to eat. Bodies and brains need calories to operate efficiently. But here's the good news: it's time now to think beyond mere nutrition. Food is so much more than just calories and chemistry. Think *variety*. The Stephanie Plum diet works because it recognizes that food is more than just simple nutrition for the body; it also provides both comfort and context for the soul.

Think about what sorts of things you like to eat. There's a time and place for tofu, edamame, and raw spinach, but none of these is likely to be a prime piece of your diet triangle. Diets don't work if you refuse to eat the official approved foods. That's why the Stephanie Plum diet consists entirely of foods that you will actually *eat*. Foods that you will enjoy eating. Food that's tasty, and also easy to find.

You don't have to be a gourmet chef—or even a semi-competent cook—to obtain the ideal foods. Forget worrying about whether you own a meatloaf pan or a pasta maker. Gorge yourself silly on take-out, coffee, and doughnuts; meatball subs and beer; ice cream; fried chicken and a side of slaw. After all, it's only logical. If you weren't supposed to eat pre-cooked or packaged food, there wouldn't be microwave meals, or delis, or pizza joints, let alone entire constellations of fast-food chain restaurants, all readily available in even the smallest of towns.

Top Five Take-Out Meals for Triangle Dieters On the Go

pizza & beer
burgers & fries
fried chicken (extra crispy)
submarine sandwiches
Chinese

The next thing many fancy diets want you to worry about is your so-called "meal schedule." These diets map out your food consumption like a military campaign: a skimpy cottage cheese and black coffee breakfast, a lunch salad with no dressing, and a skinless chicken breast dinner, all in pre-weighed portions, with a couple of nasty high-fiber snacks thrown in, and nary a doughnut in sight.

You and I know that kind of eating couldn't keep a gnat alive, let alone a human being with your chaotic schedule. Here in the real world, we have to eat meals when we get the chance, not just when the clock says we can. What are you going to do, stop chasing a fleeing FTA just because some fancy diet book says it's time to sit down and have two servings of protein and three of carbs? Does that diet book pay your rent? Of course not! So don't let it rule your life.

A good rule of thumb—or stomach—is to fit the meal to the time and place. Don't bother planning big shopping trips to stock up on raw materials or basic foodstuffs. Unless you are happy working at a stove, and have the time to cook everything from scratch, don't sweat it. Today's hectic work schedules demand flexibility. You never know when you'll have to drop everything to chase down a car thief or drive your grandma to the local funeral home for a viewing (which, by the

way, can be a handy source of tea and cookies). And why bother buy-
ing a bunch of fresh fruits and vegetables when they're just going to
turn to sludge in your refrigerator bins before you get around to eating them all?

Big shopping trips are also an inefficient use of time, since most local grocery stores, like convenience stores, now keep expanded hours.
This makes it easy to pop in for what you need when you need it.

Don't worry about having empty cupboards. The only necessities
you really need are items like ketchup and mustard, olives, peanut
butter, Pop Tarts, and coffee. These durable foodstuffs have the advantage of lasting nearly forever without going bad. Packaged cookies, chips, dips like salsa, as well as bread, ice cream, and cold cuts,
can be bought as needed, often in sizes which are just right for the
solo diner on the run. If you must read the labels on your food, ignore
the "portion size" information printed on the package's nutrition label. Those numbers are usually scaled for midgets and children, not
normal people. Your body measures food by volume, not calories. A
bag of chips takes up just as much room in your stomach as a green
salad; you decide which one you'd rather eat.

Dining with your parents is another good way to get the calories
you need while still remaining available on a moment's notice. This
path also offers the advantage of a full high-energy, three-course meal
that tastes 100 times better than anything you currently know how
to prepare—if you had the time to cook in the first place. In addition,
there are no dirty dishes to wash.

Sure, it can be embarrassing to share the table with your folks—
the interrogation about your job, your friends, or your love life; comments about your clothes, hair, and general lack of appropriate fashion
sense—but home-cooked roast chicken or pot-roast, mashed potatoes with gravy, and pineapple upside-down cake are worth it...es-
pecially when you factor in the leftovers you'll get to take home.

Another situation which can crop up is the stake-out. Stake-outs
last until you run out of patience, food, or spare room in your blad-
der. Stake-out foods are items that keep you and your stomach busy
when you have to park your butt someplace, while still staying prepared to drop everything and give chase at a moment's notice.

> ## Top Five "Stake-Out" Foods
> Tastykakes Butterscotch Krimpets*
> Snickers Bars
> deli sandwiches or subs
> chips
> burger & fries
>
> *other snack cakes may be substituted, with preference given to regional varieties

Exercise

It's no surprise that, for many people, exercise is the hardest, least enjoyable part of any diet. Taking a walk on a gorgeous day is a treat; going running and throwing up after the first half mile is about as much fun as an emergency trip to the dentist—especially if you're running with a friend who's already in fantastic shape, and especially if that friend can, and will, run rings around you while you stop to pant and choke. The key to fitting exercise into your daily routine is to make it part of your life rather than something *extra* that you *have* to do. As with selecting food, your exercise choices should be both efficient and practical. For this reason, the exercise leg of the Stephanie Plum diet triangle stresses *unintentional* rather than *intentional* workouts.

What's the difference? Intentional exercise includes all those physical fitness routines which require schedules and athletic equipment and health clubs. Many so-called sports such as running or jogging can actually be bad for you (recall the aforementioned throwing up; also, loose shoe laces can lead to tumbles). An additional consideration is that only people who are already in shape actually look good while performing intentional exercise. Unless you are a model, a superhero, or an actual athlete, you'll sweat, your hair will become disheveled, and your face will get red and blotchy. Also, Lycra, Spandex, and other snug-fitting, "stylish" exercise wear will make you look like a sausage, to say nothing of the problem of those annoying bulges—particularly that little roll just above the waistline of your shorts.

One of the beauties of unintentional exercise is that you don't need fancy clothing or gear to do it. There are as many ways to get it as there are things on your to-do list—even more, if you want to get creative. One of the first things you can do also happens to be recommended by many other weight-loss plans: get a dog. Daily walking, ball-playing, and other exercise of your pet, as well as cleaning up occasional accidents, will burn hundreds of calories and help build your stamina, as well as lowering your stress levels.

If you live in an urban area and own a car, truck, or SUV, it would also be a good idea to trade it in for a used vehicle with a poor repair record. Lemons break down frequently, giving you many opportunities to exercise by walking to all your destinations until the car is repaired or you can arrange other transportation. This type of low-stress aerobic activity is also easy on your joints and muscles. If you are lucky enough to own a vehicle which explodes, catches fire, or undergoes some other catastrophic failure, you can look forward to plenty of additional exercise while running away to evade the flying debris.

You might need to change jobs to achieve your unintentional exercise fitness goals. Working at the button factory can pay the bills and get you health insurance, but it won't challenge your mind or your body. If you chose the right job, it should be a simple matter to come up with challenging and unintentional exercise routines. Door-to-door salespeople know the joys of canvassing neighborhoods while carrying weights. Hiking block by block, up and down the street, one house at a time, will build stamina as well as giving arches and Achilles tendons a solid workout. If you're a bounty hunter or cop, add Dumpster diving for clues, as well as climbing handy trees, walls, chain-link fences, and rickety fire escapes to observe suspects. Excitement as well as exercise comes in chasing down and wrestling bail jumpers; you'll find that even the occasional mud wrestling match will increase your fitness level by incredible amounts. And just between you and me, effecting entry to (a.k.a. breaking into) a suspect's home to search for evidence can also be a major source of demanding exercise.

As a "last resort," nothing burns calories like running for your life. Defying death and escaping from captors should generally be kept to a minimum—for insurance purposes, if nothing else—but when practiced regularly, this kind of activity truly helps keep your body agile and strong. There's nothing like the rush of pure adrenalin and other stress hormones associated with the "fight or flight" response to go through those calories fast.

Attitude

The third leg of the triangle is often the most difficult to understand or quantify, and thus the hardest to adopt. Whether you want to call it attitude or mind-set, or even your "angle of attack," this piece of the triangle is inextricably tied up with body image. Everyone—from wrinkled grandmas to bad-ass bounty hunters, to cross-dressing rock musicians—worries about their appearance; some of us more than others. That's normal. But appearance is really a very small part of attitude, and it's the last thing you should let yourself get hung up on. If you do, you're likely to find yourself bawling your eyes out and stuffing your face with Cheese Doodles when you should really be buckling down to more appropriate actions. And trust me: it's damned hard to project attitude when there's mascara running down your cheeks and orange Cheese Doodle dust all over your fingers.

The first rule of Attitude Maintenance is to find something about yourself to be proud of. When you figure out what that is, stick to it. Consistency and self-confidence are the goal here, not glamour. Attitude gives you strength. It projects a warning to others that you will not take shit from anyone, that no matter what life throws at you, you can deal with it—whether you've just learned your boss has handed one of your tasks to your worst enemy, or you must confront a drunk-and-disorderly bail-jumper, or simply defy a pissed-off boyfriend.

Clothing can certainly help project attitude. Some swear by the color black: black shirts, boots, jeans, leather jackets, even vehicles. The "Jersey Girl" look—teased-up hair, tight clothing, and multiple layers of mascara—can project a sense of innate toughness. Or you might be more the miniskirt and neon animal print Lycra top type. Whatever you chose, make certain you are comfortable with your look. If you can't walk the walk, you've got no business wearing those stiletto heels.

If you're still a little weak on the whole attitude concept, it's time to take deliberate steps. One way to find your path is to seek help from a friend. Dieting with a friend can give you the moral support you need to hold firm in the diciest of situations. It's best to chose someone who's pragmatic, yet still optimistic; someone you can trust. Someone who would lend you her stun gun in a pinch, or offer to drive the getaway car.

Moral support can also come from a pet. I mentioned dogs earlier, but really for this leg of the triangle, any kind of pet could do, be it dog, goldfish, parrot, hamster—anything. All that's required is that the animal be alive and healthy, and that it responds to your care in some way. The added advantage of keeping a pet, particularly a small one, is that it can't argue out loud with you, no matter how much it might disagree.

Your job also influences your attitude. Some jobs are more obviously helpful than others in giving you firm ground to stand on, but if you really try, you'll find ways to reinforce your attitude in nearly any job.

Best Jobs for Attitude Maintenance
ex-prostitute
superhero
bounty hunter
explorer
cop

Once important thing to keep in mind, however, is that even the most powerful jobs can't make up for a basic lack of character or competence. Sure, you may be a lawyer with a real live mail-order law degree, but if you spend more time making change for the dryers in the Laundromat next door to your office than you actually do practicing law, no one's going to be impressed. Solid attitude requires that if you can't be dignified, you can at least be honest and forthright with yourself and others. Of course you'll make mistakes. No one's perfect. The trick is to try not to make the same mistake more than, say, three or four times.

Putting It All Together

Nutritionists, doctors, and dieticians will all tell you that fad diets are worse than useless when it comes to losing weight and keeping it off. What's really needed is a gradual, thoughtful, permanent change in lifestyle: a change in the way you *think* about food and exercise, as well as in the way you eat. The Stephanie Plum diet plan fulfills those needs, and more. By linking food and exercise to attitude, with equal servings of all three, you will gain a firm foundation to support your new life: a foundation which, like construction in earthquake-prone areas, allows for the shifting of the ground under your feet. With this kind of flexibility you can count on being prepared for anything. You'll be in the wind, not just ready for new experiences and challenges, but *eager* to meet them.

CHARLENE BRUSSO is a New England-based freelance writer and science fiction/fantasy author with a B.S. in physics and astronomy from the University of Rochester. She has written for Ben-Bella Books's *Farscape Forever!*, as well as an array of magazines and venues, from Amazon.com and *Amazing Stories* to *Publishers Weekly* and *Playgirl*. As Tastykakes are not available in her neck of the woods, she swears by Chocolate Clouds and Key Lime Cheesecake from Trader Joe's.

PINEAPPLE UPSIDE-DOWN CAKE

WHY STEPHANIE ALWAYS GOES BACK HOME

Candace Havens

We know why we like seeing Stephanie's family: they're hilari-
ously dysfunctional, and besides, you never know when Grand-
ma Mazur will accidentally shoot something. The question is,
why does Stephanie?

WHOEVER SAID YOU COULD never go home again obviously hadn't met Stephanie.

The Trenton, New Jersey, bounty hunter visits her parents' two-story, yellow duplex at least once a week. Some weeks it's for a good meal and a sugar fix; other times she needs information. Then there are days when she just needs to be with them, even though these people drive her crazy.

While she'd probably loathe admitting it out loud, family is important to Stephanie Plum. That's why we almost always meet her kin and travel at least briefly to the Burg in the first twenty-five pages of every book. It's the moment we all discover that she's just like the rest of us, and that's what makes her character so relatable.

I have an eccentric family myself. Stephanie has her wannabe gun-slinging Grandma Mazur who wears neon colors and flirts with men a third her age. I have Harley-riding Grandma Helen, who gets her hair done every week, just in case she meets "someone special." She's eighty-six.

Stephanie has a father who hides behind the newspaper, mumbles a great deal, and retreats to the bathroom when crises hit. This is a familiar ritual in my parents' home. My dad is a great guy, but when things get tough, the tough head for the toilet.

The bounty hunter also has a passive-aggressive mother who, de-spite wanting Steph around, never approves of her looks, job choice, or anything else for that matter—she wishes Steph would get a job at the button factory, and find a decent man. Preaching to the choir here. Except for the button factory, I can totally relate. (In between writing jobs I did a short stint as a bartender and my mother told all her friends that I was unemployed. That was preferable to admitting that I was slinging drinks for a living.)

And I'm not alone. Almost everyone has a weird Uncle Al, who makes the holidays miserable for everyone involved. Or a senile great aunt who hides all the knives before a big meal so the kids can't get hurt. There isn't a person I know who doesn't have a family they think is weird in some way.

There are the arguments, the petty jealousies, the topics of conversations which never should be discussed at the dinner table—politics, religion, pre-marital sex. (I learned that last one in a very embarrassing way courtesy of my in-laws.) For Stephanie, it's the same thing. Her never-talk-about topics include her job and love life. Unfortunately for her, those two things are often spotlighted at the most inopportune moments.

So, why, when these people drive us bonkers, do we still feel the need to go home? There are some basic reasons we endure the trials our families put us through and Stephanie shows them to us in every one of her adventures.

I've outlined them here so the next time we have a nervous breakdown after the Christmas holidays, at least we'll know why we put ourselves in the situation in the first place.

Food

While Stephanie thinks about food a lot, she never has any in her apartment, and she rarely dines out unless she's on a date or running through a fast-food joint for her friend Lula. It's a wonder her pet hamster Rex can survive on the crumbs of food she has left in her apartment. The only times we see her eat anything you can't pick up at a drive through are when she visits her parents.

When we first meet the Plums in *One for the Money*, writer Janet Evanovich tells us everything we need to know about the family dynamics in a few paragraphs. As soon as they sit down at the table Stephanie's mother begins harping on the men, or lack thereof, in her daughter's life. The trend continues through the rest of the books: Stephanie's mother never approves of her daughter's clothes, hair, or (most certainly) her choice of professions. But the younger Plum endures her mother's incessant nagging—because there's always dessert at the end of the meal.

Pot-roast and potatoes are Plum staples, but it's usually the desserts that make the bounty hunter salivate. One bite of her mom's pineapple upside-down cake and all is right-side up in Stephanie's world. It's more than a sugar rush that she gets from her mother's sweets. (In *Twelve Sharp* she tells us dessert is important because it's the base of her food pyramid.) Sometimes a girl needs more than a Tastykake or a plump jelly doughnut, and only a mother's pineapple upside-down cake will do. When she's confused, hurt, upset, or scared, like many of us, the bounty hunter turns to food. For her, the best food comes right out of her mother's kitchen.

For a lot of people food equals love, and that's true for the Plum family. No matter how much Stephanie's mother may nag, there's nothing she likes better than having her entire brood around the table for dinner. Most of the time when Steph leaves the house, she does so with containers of leftovers. It's a way her mother can send her love out with her daughter as she goes off to catch the big bad criminals. Thanks to her, Stephanie is, if not safe, at least well-fed.

In *High Five* Steph says that her mother's smell is roast lamb and red cabbage and it's not an insult. These are smells she loves, smells that give her a sense of home. Food rituals are also a big thing with the Plums. Every night at six sharp, there is a full meal on the table. And every Sunday after church, Stephanie knows that her mother is going to bring home a white bakery bag filled with jelly doughnuts. It's just the way things are done. It's that sense of stability food represents, when her world is chaotic, that sucks Stephanie in.

Stability, and also familiarity. There's a sense of comfort in familiar foods and in the fact that, though these people are nuts, they are nuts in a way Stephanie knows. When her husband had sex with another woman on Steph's dining room table, the rug was pulled out from underneath her. Then she lost her job as a lingerie buyer. She could no longer count on her marriage or her job. Those safety nets were gone. The one thing she could count on, the only thing that didn't change, was her family—and those six o'clock dinners.

Weekly Entertainment

Sometimes the meals provide nothing more than entertainment, and Grandma Mazur is always happy to contribute—from the time she shot a hole in the chicken (one of the funniest, finest moments ever written in fiction) to her warbling a Rolling Stones song while dancing around the kitchen with her iPod, Grandma M. is always good for a laugh. She's good for breaking tension in conversation, too. Most often when Grandma M. pulls her crazy antics, there's a big pause and then everyone tries to carry on like nothing absurd ever happened.

Grandma is always looking to try out new careers, such as singing in a rock 'n' roll band in *Twelve Sharp* (which she has to give up because all of the "wiggling" gives her a backache). She later talks about perhaps becoming a piano bar singer so she can wear a slinky dress with a slit up the side.

There's also Steph's niece, Mary Alice, who thinks she's a horse, and Stephanie's brother-in-law, Albert Kloughn, who may be the clumsiest man on earth. When Valerie asks in *To the Nines* if the bounty hunter thinks Kloughn is boring, Stephanie tells her, "He's too funny to be boring" (211). Whether he's duct taped to a chair or simply dropping food in his lap, Kloughn is always good for a little comic relief.

Even when the bad guys are hot on her tail, Steph can always find a moment to laugh with her family—or at the very least laugh at them. Those small moments of levity give her an opportunity to breathe, then she can run off to face the bad dudes with a smile on her face.

Gossip

Meals at the Plum house also serve as a place to get information about what's going on in the Burg. When Stephanie's on the hunt for bad guys from the suburbs, her family usually holds some kind of key. Her mother and grandmother are always up on the latest gossip, and know where most of the bodies are buried. And if they don't know whatever Stephanie needs, the information is usually only a phone call away.

It's the place where she finds out the financial status or the sleeping arrangements of anyone who lives in the Burg. Many times Stephanie is the brunt of the Burg gossip, but it also works in her favor when she's trying to find out something about the people she's hunting there.

There are even times when she hits up the youngest in the family, like in *Hard Eight* when she's searching for a mother and daughter and asks her niece Mary Alice about the little girl. Mary Alice tells Steph that the young girl is in her class and imparts some interesting tidbits to help the bounty hunter with her case. It's a win-win situation for Steph because she also ends up with a cookie. (The cookies are an after-school ritual at the Plum house.)

Family Ties

In the first book she tells us that two blocks from her parents' house she can feel the familial obligations pulling at her, sucking her into the heart of the Burg. Yes, these people drive her insane, but she can't stay away from them. She needs them—and they need her.

When someone in the family is missing, like Uncle Fred in *High Five*, Stephanie is the first person the family calls. (Isn't that always the way? They can nag you until you are nothing but a speed bump on the highway of life, but if the family needs you, you better be there.) And Stephanie's often called in to help her sister with her wedding or drop Grandma M. off at Stiva's for the latest funeral.

It goes both ways, though. Whenever there's any kind of crisis, Stephanie knows she can count on her family. Her father often picks up Stephanie in his taxi, whenever she blows up one of her cars. Even her sister, Val, has saved her life with her mad driving skills.

In *Two for the Dough* Grandma Mazur is frightened beyond belief, but she still manages to pull her .45 long barrel from her purse and get off a couple of rounds, saving Stephanie's life. Though she causes a huge explosion, almost killing them both, when she does it.

Family is family. We might nag, berate, and generally annoy one another, but when push comes to shove, we love and care for one another whatever way we can.

Safe Haven

Most importantly, home, for Stephanie, is a safe haven.

Steph is in that hazy time of our thirties where we should be grown-ups but we have a tendency to flip-flop back and forth between being a little girl who needs a hug from her mom and being a woman who can stand on her own two feet. The fact that she's still holding on to those apron strings is one of the reasons she's having trouble committing to Joe. She tried marriage once and failed (through no fault of her own). But she knows once she gets married and has her own family, which even she admits is inevitable, then she'll be a grown-up. For now, the most she can handle is taking care of Rex on a full-time basis. (He has to be the longest-living hamster ever.)

She would never admit the fact she seeks out danger, but she does. And she's a magnet for bad guys, which probably has something to do with her trying to track them down. From Benito Ramirez in the first book to Ranger-wannabe Scrog in *Twelve Sharp*, these are some bad dudes. There are days when Stephanie needs a place to hide, which tends to send her back to the bosom of her whacked-out family.

When Stephanie is in trouble, home is usually where she heads first. There's a sense of safety each time she pulls up in front of the house and Grandma M. is waiting on the front porch. (We've all learned that if her mother is there, too, something bad has happened.) In *Twelve Sharp* when she's trying to avoid Ranger and Morrelli who are camped out at her apartment, she moves home for a short bit even though some crazy guy is trying to kill her. She says, "Home feels safe, even if it isn't" (222).

Then there are times when she heads home to make sure everyone is safe. That happens in *Two for the Dough*, when Grandma Mazur gets mixed up in one of the bounty hunter's cases concerning the nasty Kenny Mancuso. Stephanie can't stand the idea that her grandmother might end up with an ice pick in the brain, so she moves home temporarily.

While she isn't exactly excited about the reason she's there, there is something comforting for her about stepping into her old room and finding that it looks almost exactly like it did when she was in high school. When she walks through the door with her basket full of clothing and hair gel, Stephanie's mom tells her, "I have the ironing board and the sewing machine in your room. You said you would never come home." Stephanie says, "I was wrong. I'm home. I'll make do," and she does (238). It's a primal instinct to want to protect family, but she's also preserving something that is precious to her.

Thanks to the Burg's inhabitants, there isn't much she can do, from spending the night at Morrelli's, to being attacked by the latest bad guy, that her mother doesn't hear about long before the bounty hunter would like her to know. But when Stephanie needs sanctuary the Burg is usually the first place she heads. In *Ten Big Ones* she tells us that the Burg, thanks to low-level mob members, is the safest place to live in Trenton. The Burg takes care of its own. By the same token, if you cause too much trouble, you could disappear forever.

It's in *One for the Money* that Stephanie tells us why she goes home to the Burg so often. "There was safety here, along with love and stability and the comfort of ritual" (7).

And that, my friends, is why most of us weather the family storms: because in the end, home is the one safe harbor most of us have.

Holt Medallion and double RITA finalist **CANDACE HAVENS** is the author of *Charmed & Dangerous*, *Charmed & Ready*, *Charmed & Deadly*, and the upcoming *Like a Charm* (Berkley, 2008). A syndicated entertainment columnist, Havens is the managing editor for FYI Television, Inc. She is also the author of the BenBella biography *Joss Whedon: The Genius Behind Buffy* and a contributor to the anthologies *Five Seasons of Angel* and *Alias Assumed: Sex, Lies, and SD-6*.

WHY CAN'T YOU BE MORE LIKE YOUR SISTER?

HOW STEPHANIE AND "PERFECT VALERIE" HAVE MORE IN COMMON THAN YOU MIGHT THINK

Keris Stainton

Let's face it: Stephanie's kind of a screw-up. She's the one her mother talks about over the phone to friends in exasperated tones, wondering where she went wrong. Helen Plum never imagined her daughter, unmarried, in her thirties, working as a bounty hunter. She's getting calls about Stephanie all the time now: Stephanie carrying a gun; Stephanie blowing stuff up; Stephanie shooting people. She never gets calls about Stephanie's sister Valerie. Or at least she didn't, until Valerie's husband left her for the babysitter and Valerie moved back home to the Burg. Now all of a sudden, Stephanie's life isn't looking quite so bad....

> "I am an only child. I have one sister."
>
> —Woody Allen

When Stephanie's mother asks her in *Four to Score*, "Why can't you be more like your sister?" (22), surely I'm not the only reader who winced. Poor Stephanie. No woman wants to be compared to her sister. Well, maybe Nicky Hilton does. But I bet the S-word is a sore point with Ashlee Simpson. Sisterhood is a complicated relationship that includes love, jealousy, rivalry, and sometimes even hatred. And it's probably fair to say that all parents end up making comparisons between their children and often also assigning roles that are hard to shake: good versus naughty, smart versus pretty, tidy versus messy.

"If you don't understand how a woman could both love her sister dearly and want to wring her neck at the same time, then you were probably an only child."

—Linda Sunshine

We are first introduced to Stephanie's "perfect" sister Valerie in the seventh book in the series, *Seven Up*. To begin with, Stephanie only ever mentions Valerie to bitch about how serene and, by implication, boring she is. "When we were kids Valerie was the perfect daughter. And I was the daughter who stepped in dog poo, sat on gum, and constantly fell off the garage roof in an attempt to fly" (*Hard Eight* 5). Stephanie, when comparing herself to Valerie, constantly finds herself lacking. At the same time, although she categorizes herself as a mess and Valerie as a saint, you can tell Steph really thinks she's way cooler and probably smarter than Val—because Stephanie has escaped Val's fate.

Mrs. Plum's point—when she asks Stephanie why she can't be more like her sister, remember?—is that Valerie is happily married, settled, secure. She's not vacillating wildly between two extremely sexy men. She doesn't get shot at or kidnapped. Her cars don't get blown up. Except, as it turns out, Valerie isn't happily married at all. Or rather, Valerie was, but her husband wasn't: he leaves her and the girls with no notice and skips off to the Caymans with the eighteen-year-old babysitter. Her marriage over, Valerie returns from California with her two daughters and moves in with her parents.

"Having a sister is like having a best friend you can't get rid of— you know whatever you do, they'll still be there."

—Amy Li

According to Stephanie, when she and Valerie were kids, Val always had scads of achievements to report to their mother, whereas Stephanie had only disasters to confess. This pattern continues into adulthood, with Valerie's marriage and children trumping Stephanie's bombs and break-ins on the welcome family news front. Valerie is the adult and Stephanie the naughty child.

Stephanie, though, plays to this even while claiming to resent it. As I suggested at the beginning of this essay, families often create roles that are hard to shake. And the fact that Stephanie's family continues to go along with the "naughty child" persona she has cultivated releases her to be as immature and irresponsible as she likes. Valerie is the responsible one, the good one, the provider of the grandchildren; Stephanie has a hamster she can't even feed properly (although since Rex is now approximately twelve years old, she's not doing him any harm either). All Steph's talk of Valerie's dullness hides Stephanie's ambivalence about the fact that Val is a grown-up and Steph still a child. It's an unhealthy pattern that we can also see developing with Valerie's daughters, Mary Alice and Angie. While Angie is a clone of "Valerie the Virgin," Mary-Alice thinks she's a horse.

> "A sister is both your mirror—and your opposite."
> —Elizabeth Fishel

Stephanie's resentment of Valerie leaps off the page, but to find its root, we need to delve a bit deeper into the sibling psyche. In some families—and I would suggest the Plum family is a good example—the perfect sister stands for an idealized version of traditional, compliant femininity. (Valerie is the personification of Stephanie's claim that the expectation of girls from the Burg is to grow up, get married, have children, gain weight, and "learn how to set a buffet for forty" [*Hard Eight* 28]. Except that the weight-gain only happened once her marriage ended.) Of course, we know (or at least suspect) that this feminine ideal doesn't exist and therefore we also know we can never measure up. It doesn't stop us trying though. No wonder we resent our apparently perfect sisters—they serve to spotlight our own perceived inadequacies. Stephanie says she wouldn't mind zapping Valerie with her stun gun—in fact, she's wanted to zap her for years—but what has Valerie actually done to warrant a zapping? Simply what was expected of her by her family and the Burg as a whole, whereas Stephanie is still, in her thirties, straining against these strictures. Stephanie admits she's sort of pleased to see her sister "screw up after a lifetime of perfection" (although Valerie's husband left her, so you could argue she didn't exactly screw up) and Stephanie seems to see Valerie's failure as validating her own relationship and employment choices.

"Sisters may share the same mother and father but appear to come from different families."

—Unknown

The perfect sister is in many ways similar to the traditional image of the perfect mother: the one whose loyalty, constancy, and commitment are supposed to hold the family—and therefore society—together. That's way too much of a guilt trip for any one woman to bear. No wonder Mrs. Plum keeps a bottle of booze in the kitchen cabinet, and no wonder modern women like Stephanie have a hard time tying the knot or balancing work and family. Who wants to be trapped by a societal role that you need to be drunk to tolerate? Stephanie observes that there is "probably a lot of my mother in Valerie," and she's right. Neither Mrs. Plum nor Valerie has gotten quite what she wanted from her life. Valerie craved (and still craves) security and the perfect marriage, but suddenly found herself alone and humiliated. Mrs. Plum has security and what seems to be a solid marriage, but in *Twelve Sharp*, Stephanie paints a scary picture of her parents' relationship: "My mother has a few rituals that make my father feel like he counts. And there's an underlying affection that's expressed mostly through tolerance" (220). Not exactly the perfect marriage, then, and probably as good an example as any of why Stephanie is so afraid to take a trip down the aisle with Morelli.

Even the failure of Valerie's "perfect" marriage plays neatly into Stephanie's commitment fears—if her "perfect" sister couldn't make it work, why should Stephanie even bother trying? The fact that Stephanie admits she can't measure up to Valerie in the marriage stakes shows a grudging admiration for Val that increases the longer Val stays in the Burg. Unlike Stephanie, Valerie makes a commitment and sticks with it, she makes a decision and follows through; she knows what she wants and she goes after it. Stephanie, always vacillating, both recognizes and resents this.

One area in which the sisters may find some common ground is in their experience with men. Because, of course, Stephanie was once married and her husband cheated on her too. (Stephanie caught her short-lived husband Dickie Orr polishing their new dining room table with her nemesis Joyce Barnhardt's butt.) Unsurprisingly Valerie and Stephanie respond to their husbands' comparable betrayals in very different ways. Valerie is desperate to marry again (in fact she considers any man—a flasher, a guy in a rabbit suit—to be fair game), whereas Stephanie can't bring herself to commit to either Morelli or Ranger. But Stephanie's feelings about a relationship with Valerie may give us a clue as to why Steph and Morelli just can't seem to make it work.

Stephanie claims she married Dickie because she was "in love with the idea of being in love"—that old chestnut. But that doesn't explain why now that she actually is in love, she won't marry Morelli. Stephanie also claims she can't commit to Morelli because she's "horribly attracted to Ranger" (*Twelve Sharp* 74). But we all know (don't we?) Ranger's just an excuse. Yes, she may well be afraid of making the same mistake again (even though she married Orr in haste and she's known Morelli all her life), but she's more afraid of turning out like Valerie—stuck in the burbs with 2.5 children and Meg Ryan hair. And, of course, turning out like her sister means turning out like her mother, and she's confident she doesn't want that. But what does she want?

> "I played with dolls until I was fifteen. My mother encouraged it because my older sister got married when she was fifteen, so Mom thought that the longer I stayed with dolls, the better."
>
> —Linda Evans

In *To the Nines* there's a telling (and fabulously antifeminist) exchange between the sisters in which they also finally find something they have in common. Valerie says, "I feel like I need a hero. I feel like I need to be rescued," and Stephanie admits she feels the same way (250). She wants to be rescued too. We all want to be rescued—right, sisters? No? Still, the hero fantasy is a valid one. That's why firefighters are so popular. But Valerie's new boyfriend is as far from a traditional hero as you can imagine, yet she subsequently refers to him as such ("My hero," she says in *To the Nines* following the birth of her child), proving that heroes not only come in all shapes and sizes, they also come fluffy straight from the dryer (85). Poor Albert. Even Valerie describes him as puppyish: "Sort of floppy and goofy and wanting to be liked" (*To the Nines* 250). How's that for emasculation? In contrast, Stephanie describes Morelli's body as "masculine perfection" (*To the Nines* 1) and talks about Ranger's "feral sexuality" (*Ten Big Ones* 120). If I were Valerie, stuck with the puppy while my sister was off having growly sex with a couple of wolves, I'd hate her guts. In fact, when Grandma Mazur questions Morelli's sexual prowess, Morelli is horrified, but Valerie laughs. Who can blame her?

Unlike Stephanie, who appears to crave freedom (without ever actually going anywhere), Valerie is so desperate for security that even though she isn't sure she wants to marry Albert she goes ahead with the wedding plans. Or rather, she allows her family to go ahead with the plans. And when Morelli accuses Stephanie of arranging their wedding behind his back, we see the same tendency in Stephanie: Stephanie isn't arranging their wedding at all, she's just allowed her family to take over the same way they do with Valerie. (In fact, there is no wedding; Stephanie just told them there was to get them off her back.) This highlights the passivity of both sisters, how they each allow others to take control of things that are important to them.

I don't think it's much of a stretch to say this behavior was learned from their parents. When stressed, Mrs. Plum goes into the kitchen, smashes a plate, and returns as if nothing has happened. Mr. Plum's coping mechanism mainly seems to be muttering under his breath. There are no confrontations in this family. You can see this pattern in Stephanie's relationship with Morelli—avoidance and dodging are the key words. (Well, and sex. I bet you can put up with a lot of avoidance and dodging if the sex is great.) Eventually, and even though wedding preparations have been made, Valerie breaks the pattern and she and Albert elope—or at least try to. It's pretty brave of Valerie and I can't quite imagine Stephanie doing it. She wouldn't even admit she couldn't really play the cello. In fact, when Valerie asked Stephanie, "Would you marry Kloughn?" Stephanie's response was, "No, but then I won't even marry Morelli" (*To the Nines* 53). Every time Stephanie and Morelli get close, she pulls away. Or rather runs for the hills. Or Dunkin' Donuts. When Valerie hires Sally Sweet as her wedding planner, Stephanie immediately starts talking about moving out of Morelli's house and getting her own place. It's usually the bride who gets cold feet, not the bride's sister.

"I love my sister very much. She is an incredibly talented, smart, and impressive individual, but she had never cooked a Thanksgiving dinner in her life."

—Mary Cheney

Morelli doesn't understand Stephanie's fears: "I don't get it. Other women are happy to stay home. My sister stays home. My brothers' wives stay home. My mother stays home. My grandmother stays home" (*Ten Big Ones* 122). Yes, and Stephanie's mother stays home. And Valerie stays home. By the very next page Stephanie and Morelli are fighting and Stephanie moves out. Yep, smooth moves there, Morelli. You couldn't have scared her off quicker if you'd given her a Meg Ryan haircut in her sleep. Morelli's Grandma Bella is disapproving of Stephanie's relationship with her grandson for similar—and yet different—reasons: "A respectable woman would be married and have children by now. You go to his house and tempt him with your body and then you leave" (*Ten Big Ones* 52).

Ah, so if Saint Valerie is the Madonna, Stephanie's role is clear. This is reinforced in *Ten Big Ones* when, as Valerie's wedding is being planned, Stephanie becomes noticeably sexier (and gets into even more trouble than usual). Stephanie is staying at Ranger's place and using his shower gel. Grandma Mazur comments that she smells "sexy" and Stephanie admits she's in love with herself. Plus there's a gang after her—her life seems genuinely to be in danger. Contrast this with poor Valerie and her giant white dress, which inspires Albert to dream of being suffocated by a whale. Valerie has a brief flirtation with switching sides—in more ways than one—when she tries on the whore role by becoming a lesbian, but it doesn't work out. Well, it couldn't really, could it? Valerie's been groomed for the Madonna role from an early age. She's about as likely to become a lesbian as she is a horse.

"The mildest, drowsiest sister has been known to turn tiger if her sibling is in trouble."

—Clara Ortega

Stephanie's passivity and commitment phobia also extend to her career. While she has been a bounty hunter over the course of the whole series, she often fantasizes about quitting, not just because it's a dangerous job but because commitment itself is hard for her. No wonder, though, when you look at her alternatives. Her mother seems to think the only viable career for a woman outside the home is an assembly line in a button factory. None too palatable for a girl who craves adventure and variety.

It turns out Valerie shares Stephanie's inability to hold down a respectable job when, in the Plum daughter tradition, Valerie gets fired on the first day of her new job in a bank after getting into a fight with her boss in *Hard Eight*. Stephanie's response to Valerie's job loss is amazement that Val actually fought with someone—it's so not Saint Valerie. Later, when Valerie is caught climbing out of the house to see Albert—just like Stephanie used to do when they were kids—Stephanie starts to realize Valerie perhaps isn't as perfect as she always thought. Finally, Valerie is kidnapped and—though clearly terrified—manages to go on and rescue Stephanie. Faced with the evidence of adult Valerie's time in the Burg, during which she proves herself to be resourceful, brave, down-to-earth, and potty-mouthed, Stephanie seems to accept that the perfect, saintly, boring, one-dimensional Valerie may never have really existed, and this realization could be enough to lead Stephanie to an understanding that their roles aren't set in stone. If Valerie doesn't have to be perfect, then perhaps Stephanie doesn't have to be a failure. If Valerie failed at marriage, maybe Stephanie could succeed.

"Lord help the mister who comes between me and my sister."

— from "Sisters" by Irving Berlin

Though their differences are clear, ultimately Stephanie and Valerie share the same survival instincts. Stephanie may be the one who escapes from burning cars and gun-toting maniacs, but she's also the one who runs away from what she really wants in the shape of Morelli (and, um, Ranger). And what about Valerie? Here's a woman so desperate to give up her freedom and choices, she'll marry a clown. Sorry—Kloughn. Is this the perfect sister we're supposed to be or at least aspire to? Yes, no, maybe. After the sudden end of her marriage, Valerie may have been desperate for a man (any man!) but that's because she knows what she wants—security, a husband, a father for her daughters—and she intends to get it, whether or not her socks are rocked. And we can't all be commitment phobes like Stephanie— if we were, the human race would disappear. There has to be a middle ground, and I think that's the message Evanovich is putting across by going to comic extremes. When we see our alternatives writ large, it's easier to find the middle ground. Freedom and commitment. Perfect and imperfect. Pineapple upside-down cake and doughnuts.

> "What the hell kind of a life do you lead? This isn't real.
> This is fucking television."
> "Wow, Val, you said fuck."
>
> —Janet Evanovich, *Hard Eight* (323)

KERIS STAINTON is a freelance journalist who has written for publications as diverse as *CosmoGIRL!*, *Mslexia*, *Scarlet*, *Practical Parenting*, and *The Daily Express*. She also co-edits women's fiction reviews and news site Trashionista (www.trashionista.com). Thanks to confiscation of her precious *Gilmore Girls* DVDs, she has finally finished a novel and is hoping it will be published . . . one day. Keris lives in Lancashire, England, with her husband and three-year-old son. You can almost always find her at www.keris-stainton.com. (If she's not there, check the TV room or the kitchen.)

RANGER AS...HAIRY GODMOTHER?

A TONGUE-IN-CHEEK LOOK AT RANGER'S ROLE IN THE STEPHANIE PLUM BOOKS

Karen Kendall

> *Ranger doesn't look like your average Fairy Godmother. No wings, for one thing. And, as Stephanie's been in a position to see firsthand, Ranger's all male—there's nothing motherly about him. But look past all that, Karen Kendall says, and you start to realize that the vanity plate on Ranger's Bronco might as well read "Bibbity Bobbity Boo."*

I. Flexible Archetypes in the Stephanie Plum Series

In beginning a project, every author of fiction creates her characters from the basis of an archetype, whether consciously or unconsciously. An archetype is (in general terms) a prototype or sketch of a character, which the writer then builds upon to make that character original. Think of it as fleshing out a stick figure. According to Tami Cowden, Caro LaFever, and Sue Viders, authors of *The Writer's Guide to Heroes and Heroines*, these archetypes can be categorized as either "core," "evolving," or "layered," depending on each character's individual personality, journey, and function.

A core archetype "fits wholly within the frame of a single archetypal description, and remains consistent in nature throughout the course of the story." An evolving archetype "begins the story as a member of one archetypal family, but is so changed during the course of the story that she...[shifts] into another." And "a layered archetype combines attributes of two archetypal descriptions" (98–99).

It's up to the author to determine which kind of archetype to employ, whereupon she will continue to shape her character and breathe life into him.

Janet Evanovich uses layered archetypes in her Plum series to fascinating effect. While Stephanie is undoubtedly the hero of Evanovich's Plum series, she also embodies anti-hero and underdog qualities. We don't take her entirely seriously, as we would a traditional hero. First, she's doing her job for the money, not social justice or world peace. Her biggest ambition seems to be ownership of a sweet car, one that won't get blown up or otherwise rendered into scrap metal. And she's a former lingerie buyer, a big-haired, blowsy Jersey girl, not a deep thinker or a saint. Stephanie's approach to her job is funny and endearing: being a bounty hunter, she says in *Four to Score*, is "about wearing a lot of bravado on the outside when you're really operating without underpants" (317).

It's these qualities that make her resonate so powerfully with modern readers who don't tend to identify with ancient philosopher or Mother Teresa types. Yet while Stephanie is no saint, she does have a core of decency; she will not cross certain moral lines. Stephanie is full of layers and interesting contradictions.

Not only does she have a problem with killing people, Stephanie does not sleep with both Morelli and Ranger at the same time, however much she may be tempted. Even in a fairly promiscuous age where readers would more than likely forgive her for doing so, she remains a fundamentally "nice girl" from the Burg. And while nice girls no longer have to be virgins, they're certainly not whores. Stephanie may wear big hair, tight jeans, and high heels, but she isn't a slut.

Somehow Stephanie Plum masterfully walks the line between feminism and traditional female values, straddling the fence without getting splinters. Female readers identify with her spunky, adventurous attitude and with her need not to be like her mother. But we also understand her need to feel safe and protected, her hesitance actually to *use* that gun in her cookie jar. Stephanie kicks ass when absolutely necessary, but she also uses make-up and hair gel.

In *The Writer's Guide to Heroes and Heroines*, Cowden, LaFever, and Viders actually mention Stephanie by name under the core archetype category of Spunky Kid, subset Working Girl.

This particular archetype and subset, they say, "... jumps at opportunities, or makes her own ... she throws herself into her work, determined to make lemonade with the lemons life hands her. Stephanie Plum, the plucky heroine of Janet Evanovich's mystery series, seizes the day and always comes through in the end" (68).

And who's the working girl of the ages? The classic one of fairy tale lore is Cinderella, who's offered a break from drudgery to attend a fabulous ball. Please bear with me for a moment as I cast Stephanie as a modern-day Cinderella. Stephanie escapes from her all-too-mundane life of lower-echelon jobs in the Burg into her bizarre career as a bounty hunter. While it's a little more complicated than attending a ball, and she's by no means having a ball, her new calling certainly requires that she be *on* the ball—as much as she's capable! And to carry the analogy further, Stephanie is forced to learn a whole new set of dance moves in order to survive. While she has no wicked stepmother or stepsisters, Stephanie *is* down on her luck, broke, and an expert at humiliating herself—no menial house chores required. And one has to admire her willingness to seek out Prince Charming by herself in *One for the Money* (screw the passivity and the glass slipper) so that she can profit by delivering him into police custody.

And speaking of Prince—or is it Princes?—Charming, Morelli and Ranger, like Stephanie, are built from layered archetypes and so serve more than one function. Evanovich has endowed both with characteristics that usually belong to a hero: they are good-looking, hardbodied, and know how to defend themselves and those they care about. Both of them occasionally pull Stephanie, the real hero, out of a jam.

But essentially Ranger and Morelli are the equivalent of Bond girls in terms of female fantasy—a brilliant, feminist reversal of the norm. As Cowden, LaFever, and Viders note, "In...earliest fiction, the role of women was...as prop to the hero. Women were usually relegated to being the object of the hero's love" (49).

In the Plum books, the men are secondary characters, not primary ones like Stephanie. Kill her off and the series ends abruptly. Kill off Ranger or Morelli and we might mourn, but the show would go on. And surely another man, equally as good-looking and capable, would appear to heighten sexual tension, rescue Stephanie when necessary, and otherwise be of convenient use.

Since we have Stephanie in the title role of Cinderella, let's now consider Morelli for the role of the reluctant and flawed Prince Charming.

Like Prince Charming, Morelli does tend to rescue Stephanie (he saves her from Ramirez-the-Rapist while she's on Morelli's trail in the first book of the series, among other such occasions).

Like the Prince, we know Morelli would scour the planet for Stephanie if she were missing. And like the Prince, he raises the expectation in readers that he will one day whisk our heroine off to his castle and they'll live happily ever after.

But unlike the prince, who is a typical core archetype, Morelli is layered, complex, and three-dimensional. He does not put Stephanie on a pedestal—in fact, he tends to annoy and overprotect her. And Prince Charming had no romantic rival for his Princess's affections the way Morelli does in Ranger.

Nor did the original prince have commitment issues. "Of course I love you. I just don't want to marry you," Morelli says to Stephanie in *High Five* (51). And it does become obvious throughout the series that Morelli loves Stephanie—that she's the only woman for him even if they don't always get along. Ranger certainly sees this, even if he doesn't mind sneaking a bite of Joe's Cupcake in *Hard Eight*. So let's go ahead and officially cast Joe in the role of hero. Where does that leave Ranger?

Ranger's archetype is the mentor.

II. Ranger as Mentor to Stephanie in the Plum Series

In the popular television series *Alias*, Sydney Bristow has her Machiavellian father, Jack, as back-up—whether she likes it or not. Dorothy, in the Wizard of Oz, gets those fabulous ruby slippers from Glenda the Good Witch. And the title character in the fairy tale Cinderella is helped along by her Fairy Godmother, who changes four white mice and a pumpkin into Cin's horses and carriage for the Prince's ball.

So let's pose the question: In Janet Evanovich's Stephanie Plum books, is Ranger Stephanie's... er, Hairy Godmother?

The common theme in each of the above stories and countless others is the mentor figure, an older, wiser, or more powerful friend who helps the heroine (or hero) through a specific quest or journey. Whether the journey is spiritual, emotional, or physical is immaterial—the function of the mentor remains the same.

As Christopher Vogler states in *The Writer's Journey*, the mentor is "usually a positive figure who aids or trains the hero....Whether it's God walking with Adam in the Garden of Eden, Merlin guiding King Arthur, the Fairy Godmother helping Cinderella, or a veteran sergeant giving advice to a rookie cop, the relationship between hero and Mentor is one of the richest sources of entertainment in literature and film" (51).

While we should probably avoid thinking of Ranger as God (other than a sex god), Ranger's character in the Stephanie Plum books does emerge clearly as mentor. In *Three to Get Deadly*, Stephanie spells it out clearly: "Ranger had been my mentor when I'd started in the business and was one very bad bounty hunter. In this case, bad meaning ultracool" (39). But his role is not as simple as playing Henry Higgins to Stephanie's Eliza Doolittle, even considering *One for the Money*'s direct references to the pair.

The first time Evanovich introduces Ranger in *One for the Money*, he laughs—at Stephanie's aspirations to become a bounty hunter in general and at her desire to bring in Joe Morelli in particular. But then he reconsiders. "This here's gonna be like Professor Higgins and Eliza Doolittle Does Trenton," he says (31).

It's a great throwaway line. However, after some initial pointers and purchases of equipment, Ranger's relationship with Stephanie is nothing like that of Higgins and Doolittle, who spent hour after hour and day after day with one another in a painstaking, whole-hearted makeover. Ranger's not exactly the pedantic type, nor is Stephanie a patient, eager sycophant.

Stephanie, the former lingerie buyer for a department store, isn't having much luck running down her first FTA. "This capturing stuff isn't as easy as it sounds," she says. "I need to talk to someone who's an expert at this job."

Connie, Vinnie's receptionist, is sympathetic. She knows just the guy: Ranger. "He makes apprehensions other agents only dream about. He gets a little creative sometimes, but hey, that's the way it is with a genius, right?" (*One for the Money* 30–31).

When Stephanie wonders dubiously just how creative Ranger gets, Connie assures her that he's like Clint Eastwood in *Dirty Harry*, and she can't possibly have a problem with Clint Eastwood, can she?

Steph's first impression of Ranger is his black pony-tail and his biceps, which look as if "they'd been carved out of granite and buffed up with Armor-All" (30). Hardly a portrait of the traditional, kindly Fairy Godmother. Needless to say, Ranger is no fairy. But soon he's agreed to give her a crash course in bounty hunting. And it's interesting in light of the Fairy Godmother analogy that one of Stephanie's reasons for responding to what Vogler would term her call to adventure (after bemoaning her crappy car and the fact that she has no food in her fridge) is that the shoes she's wearing don't fit. Is our Stephanie in need of glass slippers?

Ranger doesn't provide them, which is just as well since she's more likely to wear gym shoes—or CFM pumps on a good day. But Ranger does outfit Stephanie with her first set of handcuffs, her first gun, and her big black leather bag, as well as ten minutes of shooting lessons. He agrees to help her as long as she won't tell anyone, since he "wouldn't want to tarnish [his] image by looking like a good guy" (35).

Ranger clearly functions as a mentor, but he does so with a couple of new twists. One is that he departs from the classic mentor archetype in terms of psychological function. As Vogler says, the Mentor usually represents the higher Self or "the conscience that guides us on the road of life" (51). This certainly is not Ranger's role since he represents sexual temptation to Stephanie, not wisdom. In *High Five*, he suddenly appears in her kitchen, hot as the devil himself, while dispensing health food and lecturing her on purity of mind and body. As his eyes move over her curves, Stephanie asks, "Do you have a pure mind and body?" Ranger looks into her eyes. "Not right now" (27).

The other twist to Ranger's mentorship is born of that same sexual tension and the possibility of romance with Stephanie. Generally (though there are exceptions) an archetypical mentor does not become romantically entangled with his or her protégé. According to Vogler, mentors are more often parent-like figures. Indeed, they're often asexual and wear flowing white robes, not tight black T-shirts and bullet-proof vests. Obi-Wan Kenobi certainly has no plans to take Luke Skywalker out on a date. Likewise, Glenda the Good Witch shows no romantic yearning towards Dorothy in the Wizard of Oz. Jack is Sydney's father, so no relationship possibilities there. But Ranger breaks the mold; he definitely has romantic and sexual appeal. This is what makes him so intriguing as a mentor and, er, Hairy Godmother.

Ranger does pose the possibility of Sexual Initiation for Stephanie. (While she is no virgin, Ranger does exude a powerful sexual magnetism and threatens to ruin her for all other men.) He and Stephanie finally sleep together in *Hard Eight*, and the sexual tension remains and builds even after that.

III. Characteristics of Godmothers

I've noticed that Godmothers, whether Fairy or Hairy, do possess certain characteristics as mentors and Ranger is no exception. First, *they are secondary or tertiary characters of fictional convenience.* They are dropped into the story to serve a function, often to pass on training, information, or some other gift.

One of the biggest questions surrounding Ranger is this: Why would such a bad-ass, paramilitary, frighteningly competent bounty hunter and security specialist be working for a small-time, low-life pipsqueak like Stephanie's cousin Vinnie? The easy answer is money, but with Ranger's unlimited resources he could almost certainly buy or found a bail bonds agency of his own. So, like Glenda the Good Witch and Cinderella's Fairy Godmother, he's a little too convenient to the story.

Second, *Godmothers are of mysterious origin.* There's no doubt that Ranger fits this qualification. Part of his appeal is that for most of the books (with *Twelve Sharp* as the exception) nobody knows much about his background, except that it's rumored to be special forces, Army Ranger Training to be exact. Stephanie herself explains, "He'd been one of those army guys who went around disguised as the night, eating tree bark and beetles, scaring the bejeezus out of emerging third world insurgents" (*Three to Get Deadly* 39).

Not only is Ranger's background mysterious, his present circumstances are equally murky. He shows up regularly in Stephanie's apartment as if by magic, leaving no signs of forced entry. One night, in anticipation of his appearance, she rigs a tower of pots and pans to her front door, only to find him standing in her foyer with both deadbolts still shot and the chain still on—and no broken windows, either. He appears just like an apparition—or a Fairy Godmother.

It's also unclear how Ranger earns his seemingly limitless supply of money (Stephanie suspects gun-running) or where his vast cache of forbidding black luxury vehicles comes from. Then again, because of his function in the story, we're willing to overlook these details. After all, nobody wonders how Cinderella's Fairy Godmother achieved her magical, transformative powers. We're also content to grant Ranger his mystery because it's part of his outlaw appeal.

Third, *Fairy Godmothers possess wisdom, superpowers, or magical abilities that a hero does not have.* Ranger clearly belongs to a more mysterious realm than Stephanie. He may not have magic at his disposal like Cinderella's Fairy Godmother, but he seems to know everything and nobody can figure out how. In *Hard Eight*, as Stephanie and Lula are headed to a racetrack, Ranger calls and tells them to put money on a certain horse in a specific race. How does he know where they're headed? asks Lula. "I'm telling you, he's not human...he's from space or something" (255–256).

Stephanie often refers to Ranger as "the Wizard" and his home as the bat-cave. She notes that all of his cars are so loaded with technology that they look as if he communicates regularly with Mars.

Fourth, *mentors—Godmothers or not—give gifts, training, or knowledge to a main character, but are somewhat distant emotionally.* Again, Ranger fits the role to a T. He embodies many of what Vogler refers to as the Dramatic Functions: Teaching, Gift-Giving, and Motivation. As mentioned earlier, he trains Stephanie in the fundamentals of bounty-hunting and gives her equipment and vehicles, though they're of dubious origin. ("I never asked Ranger where he got his cars," Stephanie says in *Four to Score*, "and he never asked me my weight" [171].) The average Joe (sorry, Morelli) cannot pull a Porsche out of thin air and assign it randomly, just as the average sweet little old lady cannot turn four mice and a pumpkin into a horse-drawn carriage.

But Ranger's gifts don't make him a bosom buddy—he remains a bit distant. While Ranger regularly shows up at Stephanie's place uninvited, until the tenth book, *Ten Big Ones*, she doesn't have the slightest idea of where he stays when he's in town. (One must assume that if he told her, he'd have to kill her.)

Finally, *a Fairy Godmother exhibits heroic qualities, though she never upstages the fictional hero or heroine. And she is not a villain.* Ranger grants favors but he makes no promises. His relationship with

Stephanie is less complicated than hers with Morelli. Ranger appears, then he disappears. He gives her a car; she manages to get it blown up; he provides another. He, as noted in the series, "gets" cars, he doesn't buy them. He never files police reports when they blow up or vanish, or turns to his probably non-existent insurance company. And while Lula may joke that he'll one day demand in return from Stephanie a sexual act (probably something anal, she says) we know he never will. Any sex he has with her will be fully consensual.

Ranger is smooth, not crass; strings are not truly attached to his gifts, even though he might tease or indicate otherwise. (There you have the difference between a Hairy Godmother and the traditional God*father*, who always attaches, pulls, and exploits strings.) In *Hard Eight*, Ranger shows up at Stephanie's apartment (somehow managing to slide off her security chain from the outside), ostensibly to collect on her debt. In order to secure his aid on a takedown, she's promised him a night of his choosing, along with the activities of his choosing. After some high tension, he asks her for a non-sexual kind of favor, which leaves her half-relieved and half disappointed while he grins, reading her like a book.

One night, when Stephanie gathers her courage and asks him up for a glass of wine, he accepts. But when she drinks too much and falls asleep on her couch, she wakes next morning fully clothed. Ranger doesn't take advantage; he's a gentleman.

As a testament to Ranger's smoothness, he simply smiles when he's invited to dinner at Stephanie's parents' house, where Grandma Mazur asks about his nickname and whether Rangers are really so promiscuous that they get dogs pregnant.

While Ranger does operate outside the law, he's not villainous. As Stephanie says in *High Five*, "There was a good possibility that Ranger killed people on a regular basis. Only bad guys, of course, so who was I to criticize?" (135).

Ranger's not just a typical mercenary—he's training Stephanie for free, and it's not to do Vinnie any favors. Though he doesn't play by the rules, he has his own moral code. At some point during the series it's made clear that his money and resources definitely do not come from drug deals—Ranger is on the side of the "good guys."

Even when provoked, Ranger exhibits low-key humor and decency. Though he'll throw heinous criminals out third-story windows, when Uncle Mo (a.k.a. Old Penis Nose) steals Ranger's BMW in *Three to Get Deadly*, he is merely annoyed. He does declare matter-of-factly that he's going to have to kill him, but Stephanie asks him not to, since Mo is her FTA. Ranger asks dryly, "Professional courtesy?" And she nods (139).

Stephanie often wonders about Ranger's information network, speculating that it may involve "broken bones and small-caliber bullet holes" (141). Yet readers understand that any torture would only be administered to those who deserve it. Fairy Godmothers may employ magic or unusual methods, but they are never immoral.

Once Ranger and Stephanie sleep together, he makes her no emotional commitment and no promises. Both know that a relationship would never work out. And at the close of *Hard Eight*, that pivotal book in terms of sexual tension between the two, Ranger is gentleman enough to back off because he knows that Morelli loves her and will care for her as he can't. Here he is stepping back into the role of mentor, giving Stephanie the gift of disentanglement. He's not husband material.

Some might argue that he's acting more as hero than mentor here, sacrificing for the woman he loves. But Ranger's emotional distance is deliberate and also somewhat selfish. He has no desire to be romantically entangled himself. He is no hero, especially compared to Joe; Ranger works for money and thrills, not the greater good of the Burg like Morelli.

IV. Why Morelli Can't Be a Godmother

Now let's broach the subject of why Morelli *doesn't* qualify for Hairy Godmother status. The topic of Ranger vs. Morelli in romantic terms is someone else's, but it's fairly obvious that Ranger is the outlaw foil to Morelli's by-the-book cop.

While it's fine for Ranger to be mysterious and loaded, if Evanovich were to give Officer Joe Morelli the same characteristics and accoutrements he would become immediately suspect—a cop on the take, and therefore a certified Bad Guy. If he's a bad guy, then we cannot root for him as a romantic interest for Stephanie, because he'd be unheroic and therefore not worthy of her.

This is what makes Ranger's role in the Stephanie Plum books more interesting than Morelli's, because it's two-fold. He appears silently (almost magically)—Fairy Godmother style—to watch Stephanie's back and provide her with BMWs and Range Rovers. He helps her apprehend the bail jumpers she's after and teaches her certain tricks of the trade. He backs her up and offers a certain measure of security.

But Ranger also represents adventure to Stephanie, lending an element of danger (beyond the job) to her life—both physically and emotionally/sexually—while Joe represents safety, and home and hearth. Ranger is a Bad Boy archetype; Joe is a Warrior.

Joe can't function as a Hairy Godmother not least because he's not truly a character of convenience. He's not of mysterious origin, either—Stephanie has known him and his family all her life. Joe may possess some wisdom, but he doesn't appear to have superpowers or magical abilities in the same way Ranger does. He doesn't have the unlimited funds or the murky past.

Joe might occasionally pass along information about an FTA Stephanie's pursuing, but he disapproves of her career as a bounty hunter and certainly doesn't offer training or gifts to help.

Morelli is more grounded in the real world than Ranger is. He gets on Stephanie's nerves, he's an essential player of the Burg, and she actually does have a relationship of sorts with him. Marriage even comes up with Morelli; it never does with Ranger. After all, our heroine could never marry a health nut who makes her jog and tries to feed her sprout-and-carrot sandwiches.

Morelli is a love interest, not a mentor, and he also shares some characteristics of the hero archetype. So while Joe and Stephanie may walk into the sunset together one day, Ranger himself functions as Stephanie's Hairy Godmother... whether or not she continues to play with his wand.

KAREN KENDALL is the award-winning author of fourteen romantic comedies and many disasters. She grew up in central Texas, has a B.A. from Smith College in Northampton, Massachusetts, and now lives in South Florida with her husband, where she writes full time. The books of the Stephanie Plum series are among her most treasured possessions.

ACKNOWLEDGMENTS

Thanks to Sarah Harris and Megan Stolz for their assistance.